D0344415

Strengthening
High-Risk Families

Strengthening High-Risk Families

A HANDBOOK FOR PRACTITIONERS

Lisa Kaplan
Judith L. Girard

Lexington Books
An Imprint of Macmillan, Inc.
NEW YORK

Maxwell Macmillan Canada
TORONTO

Maxwell Macmillan International
NEW YORK OXFORD SINGAPORE SYDNEY

Library of Congress Cataloging-in-Publication Data

Kaplan, Lisa.
    Strengthening high-risk families : a handbook for practitioners /
Lisa Kaplan, Judith L. Girard.
        p.   cm.
    Includes bibliographical references and index.
    ISBN 0-02-916915-1
    1. Problem families—United States.   2. Family social work—United
States.   I. Girard, Judith L.   II. Title.
HV699.K358   1994
362.82′0973—dc20   94-4759
                                                                   CIP

Lexington Books
An Imprint of Macmillan, Inc.
866 Third Avenue, New York, N.Y. 10022

Maxwell Macmillan Canada, Inc.
1200 Eglinton Avenue East
Suite 200
Don Mills, Ontario M3C 3N1

Macmillan, Inc. is part of the Maxwell Communication Group of Companies.

Printed in the United States of America

printing number
1   2   3   4   5   6   7   8   9   10

To my parents, Helen and Matthew Kaplan, and my husband, Ron Morin, my greatest sources of strength.

—Lisa Kaplan

To my children, Tommy, Wendy, and Guy, whom I love dearly.

—Judith L. Girard

The best gift you can give any child is a parent who is capable.
—Judith L. Girard

Contents

Foreword

When Lisa Kaplan and Judith Girard approached us about writing the foreword for this book, we accepted because we're in favor of any process that endeavors to strengthen families. As we read the book, it became clear to us that their mission to inform practitioners on how to strengthen families had clearly exceeded its goal. What they have accomplished enters the relatively unexplored territory of family empowerment, encouraging families, through a therapeutic process, to take back control of their lives. It is this process of acknowledging family strengths and encouraging families to regain belief in their competency, thereby enabling them to see themselves as having power, that has us excited.

In the last fifty years we have witnessed the evolution of mental health care in the United States. The movement to go beyond warehousing patients in state hospitals to community-based systems of care has brought us more in direct contact with the problems of homelessness, mental illness, and substance abuse. The tragic consequences of the 1981 Omnibus Budget Reconciliation Act, which defunded community mental health in the United States, can be seen in the faces of the homeless in every American city. When we look at those wandering the streets, individuals and sometimes whole families, we ask, "How could this happen in the United States?" Whatever happened to the American dream? For these families, there is no dream, only a nightmare from which they fear they will never awaken.

All family preservation and support programs should be seen in the context of prevention. These families, often in a state of perpetual crisis, live from one tragic incident to the next. It is this population, which desperately needs services, that most often falls through the cracks of the community mental health system. The reasons for this are many, but we believe the real answer lies in the fundamental philosophical roots of the different missions of community mental health and family preservation. The mission of community mental health is mostly a triage function, to treat the walking wounded. However, the goal of family preservation is to treat families whose problems are so massive that they will never make it to a clinic.

The movement to embrace family preservation and support programs at the national level has spread rapidly since the early 1980s. The impact of Public Law 96-272, the Adoption Assistance and Child Welfare Act of 1980, which mandated states to make efforts to maintain children in their own homes prior to making out-of-home placements, finally seems to have been accepted in the mainstream of public policy and program initiatives for most of the fifty states. The recognition by departments of social service, which were often initially hostile to those programs, has moved to an integrated acceptance of programs that reduce out-of-home placement and have greatly reduced the need for emotionally and financially costly foster care.

The proliferation of programs has resulted in the emergence of a wide range of treatment models, from long-term case-centered approaches to shorter-term models. Our concern is that whatever the model, it needs to be family, not individually, focused. Beyond this, the quality of treatment offered and the structural integrity of the model are central to program and family success. Our culture's fascination with quick-fix remedies and magic bullet cures is harmful to these families. We have found that the real solutions rarely are the quick ones, and our limited focus may cause us to hurry past the intensive family restructuring that family preservation clearly illustrates the need for.

Kaplan and Girard's warnings concerning true collaboration, not competition, need to be heeded. We believe that if family preservation as a movement is to be successful, there must be greater cooperation and collaboration among the existing players on the social service scene: mental health, child welfare, juvenile justice, education, public health, and the various other agencies involved in families' lives.

Family preservation is often a last chance for these families in their ongoing struggle to fit into a culture that tells them they don't belong. We believe that when programs are successful, it is because practitioners are able to see the family's humanity, know their dream for a better life, and believe in their ability to achieve it. Kaplan and Girard are proposing a compassionate system of care that believes in families and in their ability to heal their own wounds.

Carl Whitaker, M.D.　　*Eric Emery, Ph.D.*
Nashotah, Wisconsin　　*Palo Alto, California*

Preface

Since the 1986 publication of Lisa Kaplan's *Working with Multiproblem Families*, the forerunner of this book, the field of family preservation has expanded rapidly and dramatically. Yet there is no core body of knowledge on working with high-risk families within a family preservation model, and there is so much variation among program models that it is difficult to obtain a thorough and accurate understanding of the field. *Strengthening High-Risk Families: A Handbook for Practitioners* is written for practitioners and administrators providing home-based family treatment, undergraduate and graduate students who want training in family preservation, and those working with high-risk families in other family-focused programs. Our goal is to encourage them to recognize its adaptability across service systems—juvenile justice, child welfare, education, mental health, health, and others.

This book begins with a historical overview of the family preservation movement and then moves on to address a number of issues being debated within the field. We recommend a pragmatic approach to family-centered assessment and treatment to empower families to change and urge practitioners not only to provide direct service but also to address issues of social change. Practitioners want to know how to work with families with especially difficult problems, and so we pay special attention to intervening with families characterized by physical or sexual abuse, domestic violence, substance abuse, HIV/AIDS, and homelessness. Additional topics covered are family reunification, dealing with diversity, and future directions and challenges for the movement. Examples are used throughout the book, drawn from cases we have worked with over the years. The names have been changed and situations altered to protect the privacy of the families.

As the field of family preservation has mushroomed, new questions have arisen. There is an especially strong need to evaluate the diverse family preservation models in order to determine which program components, as well as length and intensity of service, work best for various types of families. We must also ensure that the results of evaluation and research studies are shared with direct service providers, so that evaluation is used to guide program development.

This book is only a beginning; much work remains.

Acknowledgments

A number of people have had a significant influence on this book. We thank everyone who read all or part of the manuscript, including Marcia Allen, Claudette Ankiewicz, Dr. Eric Emery, Al Herbert, Claudia Jacobs, Marie Kearns, Darla Martin, Grace Moceri, Ron Morin, Chad Morse, Kathy Ross, Cate Scheiderich, Dr. Jessica Segré, and Dr. John Zalenski. Their enthusiasm motivated us to continue to refine our thinking. We thank them for the time and attention they gave to reviewing the manuscript and for discussing their ideas with us. We found their suggestions valuable and are profoundly grateful for their assistance. They helped make this a better book.

We would be remiss if we neglected to thank Ron Morin for the many meals he cooked, sustaining us in our work.

I am indebted to my husband, Ron Morin, for his invaluable editing, support, and encouragement. I appreciate the extraordinary amount of time he spent reworking the manuscript and helping us strive to choose the right word to get our meaning across. My husband's faith in me is a strength I couldn't do without. His own writing has been an inspiration.

I especially acknowledge Dr. Eric Emery, whom I consider part of my family. Over the years, he has given me personal and professional support; his energy and enthusiasm are seemingly inexhaustible, and his confidence in me and in my work are truly a gift.

I extend special thanks to James Allen, Karen Gincott, and Joan Newton for their continual encouragement to persevere.

Lisa Kaplan

I am greatly indebted to all of the families I have worked with over the years who have shared their lives with me. They have taught me so much.

I am especially grateful to Dr. Abe Avesar, whose strong belief in me encouraged me to do more than I ever thought I could. He made me realize that my caring and commitment to families would be the basis for all my work. My memories of our numerous conversations still inspire me.

I thank my husband for putting up with an absent partner, for even when I was physically present, my thoughts often were elsewhere. I appreciate his taking care of things so that I could focus my energies on the book. My children, Tommy, Wendy, and Guy, gave me support and encouragement, and I thank them.

My staff—Grace, Kathy, Karen, Jan, Linda, Grace, Doris, Cate, Bonnie, Barbara Jean, Kristi, Peg, and Carly—kept the program going even when I was sometimes unavailable. I appreciate their understanding and support.

Judith L. Girard

Introduction

The core premise of family preservation is that we cannot help children until we help their parents. To change the lives of children significantly, we must acknowledge that working with parents is productive and develop relationships with them.

To qualify for services, parents must fail. Families have to be at risk of losing their child before they can get assistance. Our nation's service system is predicated on the belief that intervention should occur only when parents can no longer provide a stable environment for their children. As dollars become tighter, only families with severe problems are eligible for services.

Family preservation programs can play a critical role in systems reform. They are not a panacea but rather one component in an array of services along a continuum, from family support through family preservation, ". . . the development of family preservation programs should not eclipse the need for other service options for families, including better foster care."[1] We need to implement a family-focused approach throughout the service delivery system.

A Culture of Poverty and Oppression

"There are more poor children in America today (14,341,000)," said the Children's Defense Fund in 1992, "than in any year since 1965 despite the net 88 percent growth in our Gross National Product."[2] Poor families face unemployment, substandard housing, lack of food, and inadequate medical care, as well as crime and violence, which destabilize neighborhoods. All of these factors have a powerful impact.

Poor parents worry about feeding their children, buying clothes for their children, and are constrained from taking their children on outings because they lack money and transportation. These parents are continually anxious, apprehensive, and tense, and they are often emotionally unavailable to their children. Parents who can afford a baby-sitter have the opportunity to get out and socialize. These parents are able to meet their own needs, and when they return, refreshed and energized, they can respond to their children's needs. Poor parents can never escape from relentless daily stresses. Thus, "Public policies targeted towards helping children must consider and include the needs of parents. . . . Programs targeted to at-risk children and families are most successful when those programs focus on the parent."[3]

Like the culturally different, the poor are an oppressed culture; they are stereotyped and discriminated against. People of color who are also poor suffer twofold. "The United States is the most ethnically diverse nation in history, but this fact has not increased our ability to tolerate differences."[4] We must rethink our counseling practices, acknowledge the damage they have done to the culturally different, and make more than a token commitment to increase the sensitivity and cross-cultural competence of agencies and practitioners. Cultural competency, the ability to respond to the unique needs of people whose cultures are different from the dominant culture, must be built into the foundation of our thinking and the way we do business. For too long we have failed to consider cultural competency a priority. Many social service agencies operate in a crisis mode. Emergencies receive immediate attention, while issues like cultural competency, pressing but never an emergency, get lost in the shuffle. We must embrace the importance of valuing and respecting cultural differences, ethnic differences, and life-style differences.

Our work must mobilize us to address issues of poverty, racism, and discrimination, recognizing the role of the environment and other external factors on families. We can no longer afford *not* to get involved in issues of social policy. Our effectiveness is limited by exclusively doing family work while ignoring the larger world in which families live.

Believing in Families

Adopting a family-centered approach necessitates reevaluating and rethinking the way we intervene with families. Family-centered work is a mind-set or way of thinking about families, not simply a set of techniques. Any training in this field will be irrelevant if the counselor lacks the conviction that families can change and is unable to impart this belief to families. A genuine respect for families and the ability to develop a partnership with them gives families hope and motivation to change.

A family-centered approach rests on a belief that the best place for children is with their family as long as the children's safety is not compromised. Society must demonstrate that it values families by radically altering the premise on which many social services are based, moving from "replacing families to supporting and strengthening" them.[5] We must look beyond exemplary or pilot programs scattered here and there, ensuring that family-centered values become firmly embedded in the service system, with family support, preservation, and reunification integral and permanent parts of service delivery. Finally, we must reconceptualize placement so that residential and foster care are family centered and are conceived of as a means to keep families together.

Strengthening High-Risk Families

1

The Family Preservation Movement: A Historical Overview

The family preservation movement grew out of a number of forerunners: the settlement house movement, research and treatment projects in the 1950s focusing on multiproblem families, Head Start programs, and family systems theory. Family-based services, united by a common philosophy, began in private agencies and were later adapted by public agencies. Federal and state legislation has played a role, too, as have national and state clearinghouses on family-based services.

The Settlement House Movement

The settlement houses that were established in the late 1880s in cities emerged in response to the cultural and social confusion brought on by industrialization, urbanization, and immigration. The settlement houses became an integral part of the fabric of community life, with settlement house workers, young, college-educated social activists from diverse backgrounds, providing services to those needing assistance. Samuel Barnett, a minister in England who greatly influenced the movement, believed that social reform required personal involvement with the problems of the poor and working class. "He warned that no helping scheme would have a chance of success unless it brought the helper and the helped into a friendly, mutually understanding relationship."[1] This principle of developing a positive, trusting relationship between counselor and family is crucial to the success of family preservation programs.

Although settlement houses differed from community to community, settlement house workers held common beliefs and sought common goals: to design and offer programs to meet the needs of families and to advocate for needed social change. Thus, the movement sought to merge social reform with service provision.

The settlement houses were the earliest ancestor of family preservation

1

programs, and they left a number of important legacies. One is the recognition of the interrelationship between family and community. Family preservation programs are more effective when they address the effect of environmental stressors on families. Providing only direct service while ignoring environmental stressors limits the change that can be created. Families are better served with programs that organize communities to reduce stresses.

Another important legacy is that settlement house services reflected an understanding of and respect for the community, encompassing a recognition of its culture, heritage, and values. The success of a family preservation program is contingent on offering services that families see as relevant to their needs; transportation, housekeeping, meal planning, budgeting, and shopping, are key to both movements.

Advocating on behalf of families and empowering them to advocate for themselves, a philosophy intrinsic to family preservation, has its origins in the settlement house movement. The goal of family preservation is to help families help themselves instead of creating dependence. Like the settlement houses, family preservation programs today believe in creating a strong community feeling—an esprit de corps. Families that feel a sense of belonging are less fearful, less mistrusting, and less isolated.

During the 1920s, the settlement house movement fell victim to professionalization. As workers became professionally trained, they considered their work a career instead of a passionate calling. Training became ever more specialized, and the focus of services became individually oriented and pathologically based. Professionalism and other social factors brought the demise of the settlement house movement as it was originally conceived.

Many parts of the country are now witnessing a revival of settlement houses, the result of a push by public policymakers to establish neighborhood-based initiatives instead of having one agency serve a large geographic area. This revival entails a move to services with a generalist, as opposed to specialist, thrust. It also responds to the utility of having many services under one roof.

The Family Centered Project of St. Paul

The Family Centered Project of St. Paul, established in 1947, was the first research and treatment project to focus on multiproblem families. It served these families until 1957 through direct service and community organizing.

The project began by examining four types of problems to which community services were geared—dependency, ill health, maladjustment, and recreational need—and found that 6 percent of the families in St. Paul used half of the city's social services. Many agencies had been working concurrently with these families over a long period of time, and service provision was fragmented, episodic, individually oriented, and based on the presenting problem. In an effort to offer comprehensive services, five social service agencies joined together to loan workers to the project. The project's major goals were to offer in-home services focusing on the whole family, work in partnership with families to develop mutually agreeable goals, emphasize family strengths, and have a single worker maintain primary responsibility for each family, coordinating community resources to meet the family's needs.

Each family received approximately two years of service. A study of 150 of the closed cases revealed that 65.3 percent of the families achieved positive changes, 18.7 percent had not changed, and 16 percent showed negative change.[2] Many concepts currently used in work with families today come from the Family Centered Project of St. Paul and other similar projects.[3]

Head Start

The importance of and relevance to family preservation of Head Start, probably the largest home visiting program in the country, is often overlooked. Head Start, begun in 1965 to provide preschool children from low-income families with a comprehensive child development program, consists of four major components: education, health, parent involvement, and social services. The educational component mirrors the cultural and ethnic background of the community served; in a Hispanic community, for example, Hispanic teachers are hired, and the curriculum reflects the community's ethnic heritage. A low teacher-to-child ratio and parent volunteers enable teachers to offer children individualized attention. The program emphasizes the early recognition of health problems, ensuring that each child receives medical, dental, psychological, and nutritional attention.

Parental involvement is a major focus of Head Start. The program's goal is to empower parents, encouraging them to rely on their own strengths to resolve conflicts. Parents can become involved in Head Start in four ways: making decisions about program operation; working in the classroom as observers, volunteers, or paid employees; joining in activities planned by other Head Start parents; and working with their children in their own home, with assistance from Head Start staff. Former Head Start parents comprise more than one-third of the program's paid employees, which truly reflects a commitment on the part of Head Start to empower families.[4]

Head Start's philosophy thus embodies many of the principles on which family preservation programs are based:

- Treating families with dignity and respect and encouraging the development of self-esteem among family members.
- Developing a trusting relationship with families, instilling in them a trust in themselves and in their ability to influence their world.

- Recognizing the importance of providing a comprehensive array of services to the entire family, addressing health, educational, vocational, and social needs.

- Acknowledging that parents know more about their children than anyone else and that parents can have the greatest influence on their children's development.

- Believing that parenting skills can be learned.

- Assisting parents in identifying their strengths and emphasizing that they can use these strengths to resolve interpersonal and environmental conflicts.

- Improving families' abilities to identify and assess their own needs.

- Assisting families in gaining the confidence they need so that they can draw on formal and informal community services to fulfill their own needs.

- Serving as extended family for Head Start families, providing both informal and formal support.

Family Systems Theory

Family systems theory, especially structural family therapy, forms another part of the background of the family preservation movement. Initially, the family therapy movement was considered outside the traditional social service delivery system because most practitioners provided individual therapy. As practitioners recognized that clients were affected by their environment, the movement gained credibility. Since then, family therapy has become very respectable and moved to the mainstream.

Understanding systems theory and terminology is critical to working with families. Salvador Minuchin's seminal work, *Families of the Slums* (1967), based on his work at a residential school for inner-city delinquents in New York, discusses the structure and dynamics of multineed and multiagency families, offering numerous case examples. This book, as well as his *Families and Family Therapy* (1974), explains systems theory and describes its usefulness in assessment and treatment.

An ecological family systems approach moves the focus from the individual to the family, subsystems within the family, and the family's interaction with the community.[5] The identified client's problems are considered a symptom or reflection of difficulties within the family, so treatment is focused on the family as a whole, with interventions directed at underlying patterns in the family and at issues that reflect the crisis. The family is considered within its social context as well because individual functioning is viewed as inextricably linked to environment. Thus, intervention goes beyond psychological treatment to address substandard housing, unemployment, financial difficulties, and other problems. It is the way the family copes with these problems that provides insight into family members' capabilities, communication styles, and limitations.

Emergence of Family-Centered Programs

There exists an array of diverse family-centered programs, all united by a common philosophy: to maintain children in their own homes without losing sight of their primary goal of ensuring child protection.[6] These programs focus on the entire family rather than individual family members, and they offer an array of assistance, both concrete and therapeutic services, through an ecological approach that recognizes the interdependence of family and community. Although these programs have a common philosophy, they differ significantly in other respects; they variously treat children at risk of abuse and neglect, emotionally disturbed children and adolescents, status offenders, juvenile delinquents, and youngsters with developmental disabilities. Programs are located in suburban, urban, and rural communities, tailoring their treatment to the needs of the population served. The programs vary as well in sponsorship. Although family-based services originated in private agencies, they have been adopted by public agencies. Public agencies with these programs are involved with more families than are many of the private programs that contract with public agencies.

Family-centered programs can intervene at one of any number of points: with vulnerable families whose children are at high risk of placement though not yet in crisis; when a family is in crisis and a child is about to be placed; when reunification occurs for a child who has been in foster care, a residential facility, or an inpatient unit; or when a homeless family obtains aftercare after having been in a shelter. They use diverse treatment models with varied theoretical frameworks, varying lengths of service (from four weeks to one year), varying levels of intensity of service (under one hour per week to seventeen hours per week of family contact), varying caseload sizes (from two to more than twenty cases), and various provider approaches (one counselor for each family or a team approach). Programs also vary regarding the discipline, education, and experience of staff, with some programs employing professionals, some employing paraprofessionals, and some pairing them.

Of all family-centered models, Homebuilders is the most widely known. The Homebuilders' model has been replicated or adapted throughout the United States; it has been promulgated particularly by the Edna McConnell Clark Foundation in New York, which has promoted it in state legislatures, public agencies, and key national organizations, such as the Child Welfare League of America and the Children's Defense Fund, providing them with funding to support intensive family preservation.[7]

Initiated by psychologists David Haapala and Jill Kinney, Homebuilders began in 1974 as part of Catholic Community Services of Tacoma, Washington, to provide home-based family crisis intervention and education. Homebuilders is the briefest and most intensive of all home-based programs. Families are referred to Homebuilders when a child is at imminent risk of placement. The program's goal is to prevent out-of-home placement through immediate intervention that defuses the crisis, stabilizes the family, and teaches family members new problem-resolution skills, so they can avoid future crises. The intervention is intensive. Therapists, most of whom have a master's degree, work with families over four to six weeks (with treatment targeted to last four weeks). They spend as much time as necessary with families and are on call twenty-four hours a day, often putting a year's worth of outpatient services into one month. Each therapist has a caseload of two families, spending up to twenty hours per week with each family. Typically one therapist works with each family, but additional therapists are available as needed.

The success of the Clark Foundation in obtaining widespread acceptance of the Homebuilders model is phenomenal. Clark has influenced the child welfare field and created public policy. Had it not been for Clark, the field of family preservation would look very different. Tension has been created because Clark has portrayed Homebuilders as the *only* model. Research studies do not support the efficacy of Homebuilders any more than other programs. Although Homebuilders developed a model that represents an innovative approach to child welfare, it has differentiated itself from other programs instead of joining in a common philosophy.

Family-Based Case Management in Public Agencies

Public agencies in a handful of states have developed family-based case management or family-centered case practice, retraining workers and refocusing their philosophy and policies to reflect this approach. They have lowered caseloads and revamped assessment and treatment forms. This is an entirely new paradigm in which to train caseworkers to assess and intervene with families. Although there is little written on family-centered case management, the National Resource Center on Family Based Services at the University of Iowa has developed a curriculum and has worked with states to integrate this approach and retrain workers.

Integrating family-centered services within a traditional bureaucratic agency poses numerous challenges. If a family-based delivery system is to be established, the agency director must be committed to the change, have a plan for building the service delivery system, articulate this vision, and translate it into action. Because the agency director sets the organizational expectation, this person must be able to articulate a vision of it to staff and then, critical to success, give a clear and genuine message regarding the importance of ongoing staff involvement in the organizational change. Instituting family-centered case practice in a public agency means shifting from a compliance orientation to a change orientation within the public agency itself and in working with families.

Supervisors too must be committed to a family-centered approach. They must model and practice family-centered principles in their dealings with supervisees, supporting and empowering them in making the transition to a family-based system. Without the support of upper and middle management, transition to a family systems approach is difficult. Indeed, "the ability of staff . . . to empower families is linked to the degree to which staff . . . themselves feel empowered."[8]

Public agencies typically have distinct compartmentalized, categorical divisions, an organization that poses a stumbling block to integrating an agency-wide family-based orientation. Each categorical entity has its own policies, procedures, and philosophies, and typically these divisions are child rather than family focused (for example, a public agency may have divisions such as foster care, adoption, child protective services, and family-based services). Unless all divisions adopt a family-based philosophy, service delivery will be fragmented, uncoordinated, conflictual, and unnecessarily duplicated.

Case managers who are attempting to understand a family-based model may express confusion about their role. Are they a case manager or a therapist? Is their goal to protect the child or preserve the family? Are these goals synonymous or antithetical? How can they reconcile the conflict between the helping role and the authority role? They may express concern about how they can work with families when they already have a large caseload. When confronted with the fact of working with an entire family, an already stressed worker may be overwhelmed, not realizing that working from a family-based model will be easier in the long run, since a systems approach offers a more accurate and more expedient framework from which to assess and intervene.

The Idaho Department of Health and Welfare implemented a successful family-based case management system in 1985; it was a radical change in service delivery that entailed involving its entire field staff of nearly four hundred. Child protection, child mental health, juvenile justice, jobs programs, adoptions, and substance abuse treatment were integrated under one umbrella. As a result of the agency's shift to a family focus, there was an astonishing 70 percent reduction in out-of-home placement, from 2,613 in 1985 to 823 in 1991.[9] The success of the implementation of Idaho's family-centered system is affirmed by repeated positive reports statewide from consumer families and direct service workers.

Federal and State Legislation

Three federal laws have principally affected the development of family preservation programs:

1. Child Abuse Prevention and Treatment Act (PL 93-247, 1974), which greatly increased the number of cases referred to child welfare agencies by creating statewide systems of reporting and investigating child abuse and neglect complaints.

2. Juvenile Justice and Delinquency Prevention Act (1974), which encouraged states to deinstitutionalize status offenders and saw the growth of programs offering alternatives to incarceration.

3. Adoption Assistance and Child Welfare Act of 1980 (PL 96-272), which had the greatest impact. States were mandated to make reasonable efforts to maintain children in their own homes before placing them out of home. To be eligible for federal funding, a state had to have a plan in place by October 1, 1983, indicating that reasonable efforts would be made for each child to prevent placement in out-of-home care or to encourage return home from placement.

The success of PL 96-272, however, has been stifled by the federal government's lack of funding and lack of commitment to implement the law. Moreover, in spite of lip-service to its goal of keeping families intact, the government in fact has allocated more money to place children in foster care than to provide family-based services that would obviate the need for foster care. In 1993, for example, states received $2.5 billion for foster care compared to only $295 million for child welfare services. And Title IV-E of the Social Security Act, an entitlement program, authorized the federal Foster Care Program, which guarantees matching funds that *automatically* rise with the demand for foster care. Title IV-B of the Social Security Act authorized the Child Welfare Services Program, a chief source of federal money to provide preventive intervention to families in crisis, but funds for this program must be allocated annually.[10] It seems that our priorities are confused.

The recently passed Omnibus Budget Reconciliation Act of 1993 (PL 103-66, 1993) reflects ongoing confusion about goals. Although it contains provisions regarding child welfare, foster care, and adoption assistance, almost half a billion less in funding than what the administration proposed was passed. Moreover, the law caps the funding of community-based family support, family preservation, and family reunification programs but not out-of-home placement. Nevertheless, this legislation is a significant piece of child welfare reform,[11] perhaps reflecting a growing understanding by policymakers of the effect of federal policies on families. Significant headway was also made on a federal level when the House and Senate Appropriations Conference Committee appropriated $4.91 million for the Family Resource and Support Program to aid states in creating, expanding, and operating local family resource and support programs in collaboration with social service agencies.

States too are beginning to recognize the importance of prevention, and some states have implemented legislation to shift dollars to the front end of the system. Forty-nine states have children's trust funds, which fund child abuse prevention programs, and at least thirty-five states have passed legislation encouraging the initiation of family preservation programs.[12] Other states have made policy changes, reallocating funding to support family preservation programs, and more than thirty states have developed some kind of statewide family-based initiative (a service lasting less than six months).[13]

National and State Organizations

Family-centered services have received a boost as well from national organizations, some with state affiliates, that pursue policy initiatives and offer resources and training. Among them are the following:

- National Resource Center on Family Based Services, which provides training, technical assistance, research, and information on family-based services, publishes a newsletter, and offers numerous publications.
- Family Resource Coalition, which publishes a newsletter, holds a biennial national conference, organizes local networks of family resource programs, educates the public, and undertakes activities on behalf of families and disseminates publications on family support. It emphasizes preventive family support programs rather than family-based treatment.
- National Association for Family-Based Services, which advocates nationally for family-based services, facilitates and supports the development of state organizations, and holds an annual conference. Since its inception in 1988, the Association has facilitated the rapid development of state associations. As of 1992, there were twenty-six existing and twelve emerging state associations.
- Family Preservation Clearinghouse of the Center for the Study of Social Policy, which strives to improve states' access to resources on intensive family preservation services by offering technical assistance to states developing or expanding programs modeled on Homebuilders and serving as a clearinghouse to intensive family preservation programs.

Summary

The family preservation movement was influenced by a number of diverse factors. The settlement house movement, which began in the 1880s, combined direct service with social change. The Family Centered Project of St. Paul, which existed for ten years, was the first research and treatment project on multiproblem families. Head Start provided educational services to preschool children and empowered parents to advocate for their families. Family-systems theory offered a framework for viewing families from a systems perspective. Family-based services, united by a common philosophy, began in private agencies and were later adapted by public agencies. Federal and state legislation played a role too, as have national and state family-based clearinghouses.

2
Family Preservation: Definitions, Goals, and Key Issues

Family preservation is not just another categorical service; it is a philosophy that is systematically important to all service delivery systems. Adapting a family-based approach requires a profound systemwide philosophical reorientation that begins by reevaluating our philosophy and values concerning families. The child welfare system, for example, in which the majority of family-based programs are found, has traditionally focused on placement to ensure child safety, with a long commitment to being child focused and deficit oriented. The policies and programs of many public and private agencies revolve around these key philosophical axioms. Shifting to a family-based system calls for a major overhaul of the system.

Definitions

When family-based programs first developed, they were called "home-based services."[1] Eventually they became known as family-centered or family-based services. For purposes of this book, we use these terms interchangeably. The term now used to refer to these programs is family preservation. Depending on who is using the term, it may be synonymous with Homebuilders or programs modeled on Homebuilders, or it may refer to all family-centered programs. In an effort to distinguish itself from other models, Homebuilders now refers to itself as the intensive family preservation services (IFPS) model, differentiating itself from programs that have adapted, yet modified the model. For purposes of this book, when we use the term family preservation, we are referring to all home-based, family-centered treatment programs.

The experts disagree on the definition of family preservation.[2] A study obtained high consensus from experts on the principles and values characterizing family preservation but encountered a fifty-fifty split on the definition, with one group favoring a broad definition and the other looking at it in

11

terms of a single program model (Homebuilders).[3] One author even goes so far as to say the term *family preservation* has drawbacks, most important among them that it specifies outcome: if the family does not remain intact, the intervention has failed.[4] In fact, universal family preservation is an unreasonable expectation; some children *should* be placed. The goal of the intervention is not to preserve the family at all costs but to provide what is best for the family and the children. Continued public support and funding of family preservation programs at the state and federal levels are jeopardized when they are evaluated solely on their ability to preserve families.

When intervening with families, it is essential to keep all options open; sometimes placement, with or without the intent to reunify, may be a necessary and valid option. Nineteen year old Tanisha, a single parent, and her three-year-old son, Shawn, were involved in a family-based program. During this time, Tanisha gave birth to a daughter, Tanika, who suffered from fetal alcohol syndrome. After several months, Tanisha, overwhelmed by the demands of caring for two children, one with severe health and behavioral problems, decided to give Tanika up for adoption. The worker continued to support and work with Tanisha around this decision. Even after the baby was adopted, however, Tanisha remained unable to meet her son's basic needs. She fed him infrequently, and then not with nutritious food, and rarely bathed him. After several more months of seeing minimal change in the care of Shawn the worker discussed the situation with Tanisha, explaining that she was compelled to report the neglect to the state child welfare agency. Shawn was removed and placed in foster care for five months. The worker continued to work with the mother around issues of neglect. Having her child removed motivated Tanisha to admit she had a drinking problem and to seek treatment. She began attending AA meetings and a parent education and support group led by her worker. In time, the decision was made to reunite mother and son based on the gains Tanisha had made in dealing with her addiction and acquiring some basic parenting skills. That the counselor continued to work in the home after Tanisha's son was removed benefited the family by providing necessary support for reunification.

Goals of Family Preservation

Despite a wide array of family-based models, all programs have a dual commitment: to protect children and strengthen families. The focus is no longer child placement but family empowerment.

Child Safety

The goal of family preservation is to provide a safe place for children, preferably their own homes. But not all families are appropriate candidates for family preservation or family reunification. Children at high risk of severe neglect or physical or sexual abuse must be placed. Nevertheless, many children currently placed would be better off remaining at home if their families received assistance and support.

A commitment to a family-based system does not mean abandoning children under the guise of helping families. Indeed, there is no stark choice between protecting children or preserving families, because the goal is first and foremost to keep children safe.[5] If a child cannot be protected within a family preservation program, then placement must be recommended. Even in placement, a child is not guaranteed safety. A study funded by the National Center of Child Abuse in 1984 determined that for every 1,000 children in placement, approximately 30 are abused.[6]

The traditional child welfare service system puts workers in the untenable position of being completely responsible for a child's safety. In a family preservation approach, the worker and family identify mutual areas of concern, shifting "accountability for future abuse or neglect from solely the worker to a balance of accountability which includes not only the worker, but the family in determining and meeting the safety needs of its members."[7] Family preservation programs focus on safety by having highly trained staff with low caseloads work with families in their homes to reduce stress. Counselors closely observe families through frequent contact so that they will know whether a child is at risk. The fact that workers are often in the home and are so visible in itself creates safety. Home-based, family-centered programs improve safety rather than inhibit it. They also serve as a valuable tool for child protection investigators, who can rely on home-based workers to obtain a comprehensive risk assessment.

Why Keep Families Together?

Loyalty to family runs deep, and a child will tolerate just about anything to keep his or her family together. Time and again, we see a child run away from foster or residential care and where do we most often find this youngster? Home. No matter how dysfunctional the family, children want to be loved and accepted by their parents. We may give up on birth families, but children rarely do, and we must acknowledge the power of the parent-child bond and understand that the best place for a child is with his or her parents as long as the youngster's safety is not compromised.

Removing a child from home is traumatizing for the child and may have a life-long impact on him or her, as well as the family, especially if the child is very young.[8] Not only is the parent-child bond severed, but the child may experience multiple placements and may be exposed to abuse. A U.S. Department of Health and Human Services report estimates that 50 percent of youngsters in residential care receive inappropriate treatment.[9] Yet children continue to be placed there because there often are no other alternative services available. Family preservation programs offer a chance for families to stay together by helping parents change.

The number of children in out-of-home care, particularly infants and young children, is growing dramatically. In 1960, 256,000 children were placed out-of-home; in 1991, 600,000 children, with every part of the country showing increases.[10] If current trends continue, the number of children in out-of-home care under the auspices of the juvenile justice, mental health, and child welfare systems may reach 900,000 by 1995. The price tag for these services is hefty. Foster care costs approximately $10,000 per year per child, and the most expensive residential care costs $100,000.[11]

Family preservation programs offer a chance for families to stay together and at lower cost than out-of-home placement—anywhere from $2,000 to $6,000 annually. These programs not only help parents change but reduce the possibility that other children in the family will become involved in the social service system.

Why Provide Home-Based Services?

Social work has a long history of providing home visiting to families, for good reason.[12] A worker who goes to the home of a high-risk family gives the family the message that he or she has gone out of the way to meet the family on its own turf. This is the first step in establishing a positive relationship. The worker is willing to step into the family's reality. A visit also increases the likelihood that more family members as well as significant others will participate. In-home services are particularly useful in isolated rural areas, prove advantageous when a family has no transportation or when transportation is difficult (e.g., a single mother having to take two buses with her three children, all under the age of ten, to meet at an office), and are beneficial when a family member is in poor health and would find travel to a worker's office difficult or impossible.

Home-based work is helpful in assessment as well as intervention. Observing a family at home can quickly bring family dynamics into focus and offer valuable information that may be inaccessible in an office setting. Grace, a thirteen-year-old juvenile delinquent, was referred to a family-based program. The worker met with Grace, her parents, and two siblings at the state's juvenile justice agency to conduct an intake. When she asked what issues the family wanted to work on, most of the responses focused on getting Grace to shape up. They couldn't think of any other needs they wanted assistance with. A few days later, the worker made a home visit and as she sat in the kitchen, having a conversation with Grace's parents, she noticed that the stove burners were on and the oven door was open. The reason: this was how they heated the apartment because their furnace was broken. The worker helped the family complete an application with the local community action agency to be enrolled in their energy assistance program. Clearly this home visit revealed important information about this family's life circumstances.

Doing home-based work answers a number of questions the worker may have about the neighborhood—is it dangerous and stressful—and the physical environment of the home—are there photos of family members? How much privacy do family members have? Does the telephone ring repeatedly? Is the television always on? Are people constantly dropping by? Are there any clues about what a family member does well (for example, drawings by a youngster taped to the refrigerator or a crocheted pillow on the couch)? Any hint of talent in the home will facilitate the worker's encouragement of a family member's abilities.

By virtue of being in the home, workers can notice family strengths that may be overlooked otherwise. A worker in a traditional office-based program may write off a family as dysfunctional because the mother regularly misses her appointments, and when she does come in, she yells at her children in frustration, trying to control their behavior. A home-based worker may draw a completely different conclusion when he sees children's drawings displayed on the kitchen walls, a clear indication that this mother is proud of her children and a strength that must be acknowledged and respected.

Home-based services enable the worker to learn about the family's culture. Workers can obtain insight into cultural values, beliefs, and practices, such as parenting, language and communication styles, family rules, couple relationships, extended family, and religious practices. Recognition of a family's cultural identity helps workers plan culturally responsive interventions.

Finally, most families are more comfortable and less reluctant to participate when seen in their own homes. They can immediately try out what they learn in treatment instead of having to translate discussions from the office to the home environment. The worker coaches clients to practice new behaviors and reinforces them.

Key Issues in Family Preservation

Family Support and Family Preservation: A Need to Work Together

Regrettably, prevention has received less attention and less funding than treatment from federal and state agencies. We claim that we are unable to find the resources to prevent an impending crisis though perfectly willing to treat the crisis *after* it occurs. Our shame is that we pay scant attention to children and their families and spend little money on them until it is absolutely necessary. Currently, to qualify for help, an individual or family is categorized, assigned a pathological label, and placed under the auspices of a state agency. This experience is dehumanizing and stigmatizing; worse, the help often comes too late. As a society, we must undergo a philosophical shift.

The field of family-based services can be viewed on a continuum, with prevention at one end and treatment at the other. An ideal goal would be to have family resource centers throughout the country, which all families could contact with questions, for assistance, and for referrals, as necessary. These centers could assist families in a variety of life cycle transitions, serving a dual role of preventing a family's involvement with the social service system and acting as a resource and source of support after a family has received family preservation or reunification services. There is clearly a need for federal, state, and corporate policies that support families. By putting energy into families up front, we intervene before problems escalate and become chronic, and we also save money by preventing out-of-home placement. The United States does not have a history of supporting preventive services, although the federal government and a number of public agencies are beginning to recognize and explore the advantages of preventive family support services.

The field of family-based services offers family support, providing preventive programs, and family preservation, offering treatment intervention. The movements claim common ancestry in the settlement house movement and have a similar philosophy and values, but they function quite independently.

Family support offers services such as family life education, home visitor programs, parent education, drop-in centers, and child care. These programs differ by mission, funding, auspices, staffing, types of services offered, and methods used to deliver them and whether they are free-standing or supplement existing social services. All have similar underlying principles and values; a local base; universal access; an emphasis on families with young children to provide parenting education and assistance; and a goal of linking families with formal and informal services and supports.

Family preservation offers services once a problem has been identified. These services are remedial, necessitating that a family come to the attention of the social service system. Family support and family preservation have thus grown up in totally different systems and are far from integrated.[13]

The differences between family support and family preservation present numerous barriers and challenges that must be overcome to achieve the goal of a family-based system of integrated services encompassing a range of support:

1. Workers in each movement speak a very different language; each movement has its own terminology.

2. Each movement has developed under the auspices of different service systems. Family support programs primarily work with communities, school systems, hospitals, and corporations; most family preservation programs are tied to child welfare, with programs operating under the auspices of public and private agencies.

3. Family support programs operate at the grass-roots level and are consumer oriented, community centered, and voluntary; participation in family preservation programs is often mandatory. Family support is

rooted in a purely voluntary service philosophy that depends on an individual's willingness or motivation to participate. As they become more involved with bureaucratic institutions, family support programs are concerned about being perceived as compulsory, having long viewed themselves as voluntary options.

4. Each relies on different funding sources. Family support programs are primarily privately funded; most family preservation programs are publicly funded. (State funding of family support programs is occurring, however.)

5. Family support programs typically work with families for a minimum of two years. Many family preservation programs intervene when families are in crisis, provide short-term services, and leave.

6. Many of those in family preservation are invested in creating a whole new class of experts and shoring up standards for those working in the field; family support is invested in a grass-roots service in which staff act as extended family.

Few programs combine family support and family preservation, so developing an integrated program will necessitate creating a totally new organizational culture. Of key importance is an emphasis on neighborhood-based service.[14] An integrated program is best designed and implemented at the community level, where it can be genuinely responsive and tailor services to meet the needs of the particular community. The Center for Family Life in Sunset Park is an excellent example of a program that combines family support and preservation services. This neighborhood program, which began in 1978, provides intensive, multidimensional, family-focused services in Sunset Park, an urban community in Brooklyn, New York. The program receives self-referrals as well as referrals from schools, social service agencies, courts, and relatives of clients. The center does not accept categorical funding because it refuses to classify individuals or families by presenting problems. Services, based entirely on the needs of individuals, are characterized by a multiple treatment approach designed to meet a broad spectrum of needs. In designing a service plan, the program considers the individual and family within the context of their environment as opposed to allocating treatment according to problem category. All of the programs use a family systems approach, offering numerous supports ranging from developmental to rehabilitative. In the center's experience, service based totally on remediation is ineffectual. The counselor takes a developmental approach and also works to improve the client's quality of life. The center's programs include individual, group, and family counseling; family life education; an emergency food program; an advocacy clinic; a foster grandparent program; a summer day camp; an infant-toddler-parent program; a big brother–big sister program; recreational activities; school-based programs for children and parents (including child care for youngsters of working parents); and an employment and job placement program. It offers an open, welcoming, nonstigmatizing environment similar to the old settlement houses. The agency is invested and involved in addressing community needs, recognizing that offering family support and preservation services without considering larger social problems is unrealistic.

The possibility of offering a continuum of services, from family support through family preservation and reunification, is gaining attention. A continuum could be available from birth on, providing preventive services as well as treatment, and offering follow-up services in the form of family support after treatment intervention. Families could use services on and off over their life span, as necessitated by their individual circumstances. On the federal level, the National Resource Center for Family Support Programs and the National Resource Center on Family Based Services have been placed under the same umbrella—the Children's Bureau—an encouraging sign representing a move toward service integration.

There is great potential for innovative relationships between family support and family preservation programs. If these movements work cooperatively and offer integrated services, they will have a powerful impact on family policy.

A Family-Centered Approach Across Service Delivery Systems

Instead of a narrow focus on increasing the number of family preservation programs around the country, our goal is to implement a family-centered approach to service delivery across all service systems: child welfare, juvenile justice, mental health, mental retardation, education, substance abuse, and public health services. This approach has already captured the attention of public agencies; Missouri, Idaho, and Kansas are developing family-centered service systems.[15]

Conceptualizing a comprehensive family-based service system necessitates determining where key decision-making points are in the service delivery system and ensuring that they are family based. Many children receive psychological evaluations that fail to consider the context of their families or their environment; furthermore, most children are evaluated in an office, not in their own home. It is not uncommon for placement to be recommended as an outcome of many evaluations. A system that is truly committed to keeping families together should offer home-based assessments systemwide, evaluating children within their families and the environment in which they live, supplemented, if necessary, by an individual psychological evaluation. Infusing a family-based focus across service systems and throughout all facets of our service delivery system is a long-term commitment.

Family-based services must be part of a balanced service delivery system that considers both family preservation and out-of-home placement; they are complementary, not adversarial. We must reconceptualize placement so that residential and foster care are consonant with the philosophy and goals of a family-based service system, envisioning placement options as a means to keep families together.

We have traditionally recruited foster parents by asking for help to "save or rescue a child from a dysfunctional family." This recruitment strategy gives foster parents the message that biological families are malevolent, implying that family reunification efforts should be resisted. Often foster parents have the best interests of the child at heart; they want to protect a child, and they often have negative feelings or attitudes toward a child's biological family. A significant change is needed here. Public agencies must alter their recruiting strategies, seeking foster parents who want to participate in an effort to keep families together. Foster families would know from the beginning that their goal is to assist in family reunification. This change in philosophical orientation dramatically changes the values of the foster care system and the way foster parents conceptualize their roles.

Some residential facilities and institutions either overtly or covertly disapprove of the proliferation of family preservation programs, angry because family preservation funding is often allocated from out-of-home placement monies. Others that formerly provided only residential programs now offer a continuum of care, ranging from family preservation programs to prevent placement to residential programs that work with families while youngsters are in placement and also reunify children and their families.

Any effort to design a family-based service system must reconceptualize group care. Like foster care, the goal of group care is to facilitate a child's reunification, when appropriate, by working with the family while the youth is in care.

Family Preservation Programs: Dangers of Moving into the Mainstream

When family preservation programs began, they were outside the traditional social service delivery system. They are now making inroads into mainstream service systems. But there is a price: The more mainstream a movement becomes, the more bureaucratic, compartmentalized, and professionalized it gets. We learned about the dangers of this from the settlement house movement. We also learned this from the family therapy movement. When interviewed, Salvador Minuchin pointed out that the failure of family therapy is related to its success. Family therapy as a treatment modality was adapted in agencies everywhere, but in many instances it was co-opted.[16] Although the family therapy movement began as a rebellious effort to question the way we conceptualize people's problems, many agencies reinterpreted family therapy to meet their own institutional needs, compromising it as originally conceived. Once the movement became part of the mainstream, it lost its fervor. Family preservation may follow in the footsteps of family therapy or in the footsteps of the settlement house movement and be co-opted.

Staffing

Because the counselor-family relationship is the key to successful treatment, choosing appropriate staff is critical. There is ongoing debate as to whether professionals or paraprofessionals, or a team of professionals and paraprofessionals, can best work with high-risk families. Regardless of a worker's academic degree and experience, however, an ability to develop a genuine relationship with clients is imperative. As a result of professionalization we are sometimes left with well-trained individuals who possess a repertoire of techniques but who do not know how to be human and who fail to see the family within the context of their environment. This is the risk we run as family preservation becomes professionalized and training becomes institutionalized. The counselor's job is not to be an expert or authority but to serve as facilitator and partner.

Evaluation

Because the family preservation field is expanding so rapidly, there is a need for research entailing rigorous experimental evaluations involving random assignment of cases to control and experimental groups. Much of the research that has already been conducted has examined the problem of determining success based on whether placement was prevented. This research has indicated promising results about family preservation programs' "ability in the short term to reduce the need for out-of-home placement and, in doing so, reduce foster care costs. However little is known about the long-term effectiveness of family preservation services or how they compare with other less intensive, traditional child welfare services."[17] Most evaluations are conducted over the short term, following clients for a year at most. We also need to evaluate the longitudinal effect of services on preserving and reunifying families.

Using placement prevention as the sole criterion for success has distracted us from examining other outcome measures, such as determining what intervention strategies work best with what types of families. "Family preservation programs should be evaluated on the extent to which they assure the safety of family members, assist in problem definition, and goal selection, and facilitate the achievement of goals."[18] Other areas of research need to consider families within their environment and determine the effect of social supports, poverty, and unemployment.

Program Length: Responding to the Needs of Families

A major controversy within the family preservation field focuses on what is more effective: short or long-term services. This may be a misguided concern, however. The family preservation movement was created to offer flexible services to meet the needs of high-risk families, so it seems ironic to impose the same preconceived time limit on every family. Families have different and varying strengths and needs, necessitating varying levels of service intensity and duration. The philosophical commitment should be based on individualizing or tailoring treatment to meet families' needs rather than on providing a prepackaged intervention to all families. Just as families are diverse and require varying interventions, so should programs be characterized by diversity, and this should be viewed as a strength. It is unrealistic and undesirable, not to mention impossible, to expect all programs to adhere to the same program model.

A focus on length of treatment loses sight of the goal of providing comprehensive services to meet the range of families' concrete and therapeutic needs. In keeping with a commitment to be responsive to families, each worker and each family collaboratively determines appropriate length of service and service intensity based on the family's resiliency and its capabilities. The question is not, How long should services be provided? Rather, it is, How much assistance and how much time does this family require to organize itself and gain new skills?

Short- and long-term models differ in their goals, and each must be matched to families. Short-term programs are designed to defuse a crisis and then refer the family to community-based resources, if there are resources available that are consistent with the philosophy of family preservation. For families with chronic, multigenerational problems and few resources, long-term intervention is the better choice. Many of these families may never have had a trusting relationship; developing one takes time and is critical to success.

Continuing Education and Academia

National organizations representing family support and family treatment provide a good deal of training and also offer publications. The National Resource Center on Family Based Services and Homebuilders provide the bulk of available training. Since Homebuilders has been so heavily promoted by the Edna McConnell Clark Foundation, this model is more widely known than others.

The family preservation field still has no national leaders to champion its causes. In contrast, the family therapy field has nationally known gurus. Additionally, despite numerous journal articles and unpublished papers, there is an obvious paucity of books on family preservation, and family preservation has not received much attention from academia.

3
High-Risk Families and Interfacing Agencies

Historically, high-risk families have been defined by their deficits. Referred to as multiproblem, resistant, unmotivated, hostile, crazy, impossible, or hopeless—or all of these words—these families have been stigmatized and labeled by workers, agencies, and the communities in which they live. Workers may use these labels in an effort to distance themselves. But these terms are demeaning and dehumanizing, and their use ultimately is insidious: "People who reflect in their attitudes toward themselves the negative attitudes of others toward them . . . [and] think of themselves as being just as worthless as others have said they are."[1] We must banish the use of negative labels because they stifle our work. Overcoming a framework of pathology and negativity that has been instilled in us is no easy feat, but working with multiple-need families necessitates working from strengths.

Throughout this book we refer to families as multineed or high risk, discarding negative terms in favor of these somewhat more positive terms, in keeping with doing family work from a strength-focused approach. The framework in which a worker views a family influences the way that person approaches assessment and treatment. Creating a language of hope and reframing the context in which we view multiple-need families are vital.

Characteristics of High-Risk Families

Multineed families typically are defined by their deficits, but they have strengths as well, which are important to recognize. (Keep in mind that these strengths fall along a continuum; some families have more than others.)

First, high-risk families are resilient. They keep going, making it through each day in the face of adversity. Second, most parents want to keep their families together. Parents may encounter a myriad of obstacles and may not openly demonstrate that they care about their children, yet most parents love their children and do not want their family separated. This love often goes

22

unrecognized. Third, the family is seeking to improve their lot. They may be apprehensive of change, however, and workers must acknowledge this ambivalence of both seeking change and fearing it. Fourth, many multineed families are resourceful. One family who didn't have enough food obtained food from the food pantry to feed their children. Another family had so many workers involved that they were overwhelmed and had their telephone disconnected. This action did not solve their problems, but we cannot deny that it was resourceful. Fifth, these families are experts on what they need. Interventions neglecting their input are destined to fail. A final strength is that most high-risk families have a healthy distrust of social service workers based on their past experiences. We respect the family's reality and their history.

By definition, a multineed family has a number of problems that cut across many dimensions of family life and cannot cope with or manage them. They face internal pressures (within the family) and external ones (between the family and the community). And although they are often referred to as disorganized because they seem to be chaotic, these families have an organizational structure, although not in the traditional sense of organized. Harry Aponte uses the word *underorganized*, which suggests "not so much an improper kind of organization, as a deficiency in the degree of constancy, differentiation, and flexibility of the structural organization of the family system."[2]

Those who live in a high-risk family always have the impending feeling that something bad is going to happen. This foreboding feeling is highly disruptive because the collective anxiety it generates distorts reality. People with unmet needs periodically explode. The perceptions and feelings of children in these families are for the most part ignored or rejected, and the children eventually learn not to trust and not to feel.

High-risk families also face many external day-to-day environmental stresses: crime, violence, drugs, substandard housing, lack of transportation, and lack of education and job training. The income of many of these families is near or below the poverty level. The more problems a family has, the more stressed and overwhelmed the family tends to be. Too often workers perceive a family's dilemmas as endemic to it and give little if any attention to the environment. If these workers address intrapsychic and interpersonal problems rather than confront pressing external problems, their attempts to help will fail.

Because workers often believe that they can have little, if any, influence on the family's environment, they focus on the family itself. Interestingly, a parallel process prevails: The worker, like the family, feels hopeless and unable to change the environment. Instead of becoming paralyzed, family preservation programs must undertake community organizing or social action. Workers fail families when they ignore or underestimate the effect of the negative, highly stressful environment in which many families live each day. Too few programs adopt a dual approach of direct service and grass-roots social reform, and even fewer get involved in or are even aware of local, state, or federal legislation affecting families. Workers can serve their goal of change by getting involved at the local level, as the settlement house movement did when it successfully merged social reform and service provision.

Multineed families tend to feel isolated. They may lack a support system to help them cope with their problems—friends, extended family, a religious institution—and often do not avail themselves of support services within their community. Most lack positive role models and distrust the outside world, having had few positive experiences, and maybe none at all, with which to build a sense of trust.

High-risk families may be overwhelmed by their difficulties, or they may be resigned to their predicament. Seeing no alternatives or solutions, typically they are negative and feel defeated, and they have low self-esteem. They often respond to crises by becoming overwhelmed instead of prioritizing the issues they need to address. Multineed families are characterized by chronicity and crisis; problems are recurrent and ongoing, not only from year to year but from one generation to the next. The family is known for its frequent crises, often requesting assistance when a crisis occurs, only to cease contact until there is another crisis.

Agencies Involved with Families at Risk

A national examination of social services for children, youth, and families in 1989 revealed that time and again only children with severe problems were able to obtain services. The researchers' conclusion was that child protective services "have emerged as the dominant public child and family service, in effect 'driving' the public agency and often taking over child welfare entirely."[3]

The national trend has been for governors, legislatures, and public agency directors to target those with the most severe problems. Perhaps this focus has come about due to federal incentives and compliance requirements, as well as media reports and our general philosophy of not dealing with anything until it is broken. A small group of severe abuse cases, approximately 5 percent of the total caseload, monopolizes child protective services and shapes service delivery.[4] These findings are provocative, especially when compared to the study conducted in St. Paul, Minnesota, forty years ago that determined that 6 percent of the families in the city used half of the city's social services. It is still a small percentage of families with severe problems who use a disproportionate amount of resources.

Public agencies separate service delivery into categorical units, yet child and family problems do not fall neatly into categories, such as "juvenile justice," "substance abuse," "mental health," or "child abuse and neglect." Moreover, many clients have multiple needs, not single problems. "The same children appear in different systems at different times or at the same time."[5] Children who come to the attention of one system are often similar to children who come to the attention of another system, and these youngsters possess interrelated problems. It "may be chance, time, or stage which determines where the child is noticed or dealt with."[6] In addition, a single family may have children in separate systems.

Michael exemplifies these problems. When he was two years old, his parents were divorced. His mother remarried when Michael was four years old, subsequently had four children, and later got divorced; his father remarried and had three children. At the age of nine, Michael began abusing drugs. Three years later, he was referred to the child welfare agency for his acting-out behavior and was placed with his maternal grandmother, who had problems too: She had been hospitalized in a state hospital, diagnosed as obsessive-compulsive. He was there only a short period of time before he was thrown out of the house. The child welfare agency next placed him in a foster home, where he overdosed on Valium. Then he spent three months in a drug treatment program and from there went to a psychiatric hospital. He continued to be placed in residential programs, where he either ran away or was thrown out. At age fourteen, he was prosecuted for stealing cars and robbing stores and was placed in a residential program for delinquents.

Michael's alcohol and drug abuse escalated. Over a period of seven years, from age thirteen until age nineteen, he had twenty-eight placements, including four admissions to a state hospital. The first admission at thirteen was for drug dependence, hallucinogens, and excessive drinking; the second for drug dependence and hallucinogens; the third for acute schizophrenic reaction and drug addiction; and the last for acute schizophrenia. Michael had still more problems; he had back surgery at age sixteen for scoliosis and at age eighteen was suffering from hepatitis. Michael is a good example of a youth with multiple needs who came to the attention of numerous service systems. He initially had behavioral problems, developed an addiction to drugs and alcohol, had medical and psychiatric problems, as well as criminal behavior.

Currently, the first system to have contact with the client determines treatment; What is needed is coordination across systems and services tailored to each family. Service systems involved with multineed, multisystem families work in isolation, providing fragmented and duplicated services that are often unplanned, crisis oriented, and organized on a deficit model, assessing people according to personal pathology.[7] Moreover, most services are uncoordinated and individually focused and may create more difficulty for the family than it already has.[8]

New and severe problems—the increase in drug abuse, AIDS, and homelessness—have overburdened public agencies. More young children under the age of five are entering care, frequently requiring specialized foster care that is often unavailable. Public agency caseloads have increased and have become more complex and more severe, contributing to the stress and the low morale of caseworkers. It is within this context that caseworkers become involved with multineed families whom they perceive as overwhelming, frustrating, and draining.

Public agencies are charged with the difficult task of transforming "a melange of categorical funds with unrelated rules into a coherent program—or at least to appear to have achieved coherence."[9] Many believe that the increase in categorical funding since the late 1970s has been the major reason for the perpetuation of a exceedingly fragmented service system.[10] States that recognize the severe limitations and the negative repercussions of their service delivery systems are tailoring services to meet the needs of the individual and family, changing an administrative structure to decategorize services, and integrating and coordinating service delivery across service systems. In an effort to integrate service delivery, states are emphasizing case management, pooled or flexible funding, and structural reorganization. They are also adopting a family systems approach, employing family support services, family preservation, and a network of services at the neighborhood level.

Some states have already changed their service delivery systems. Iowa has been a pioneer in decategorizing funding; designated counties pool over thirty funding streams for child welfare services, a system that has increased spending for family-based services and reduced out-of-home placement. Hawaii is improving service delivery to families by developing community-based centers that offer a comprehensive array of services. The centers work collaboratively with the state's neonatal home visiting program called Healthy Start, referring families to the program and offering supplementary services to those families and others. Maryland's reform of child and family services is aimed at providing family-based services to reduce placement out of home and out of state through the development of private-public partnerships. Local governing boards in twenty-four counties, composed of service providers, parents, and representatives from the business community, determine how to spend pooled funding from four state departments. Counties can keep seventy-five percent of the savings from reduced placements to use for preventive services.[11] Missouri's Walbridge Caring Communities Program in St. Louis, initiated in 1989, is a response to children living in poverty. This program, which built in cross-systems collaboration among four state departments—Education, Health, Mental Health, and Social Services—is delivered in public schools and maintains an Afrocentric approach. Services include preschool programs emphasizing early child development, basic health care services, case management, substance abuse services, home-based crisis intervention, and social services (Head Start and latchkey programs). In addition, the program meets special needs, such as child care for working parents, and it maintains a food cooperative to address nutritional needs.[12] This is a community-based family support and preservation program.

High-Risk Families and the Social Service System

The high-risk family is all too familiar with and to the social service system. It has often been involved with social service agencies for generations—perhaps repeatedly involved with a single agency for a recurring problem or with family members working with more than one agency simultaneously. This family is known, disliked, alienated, and rejected by workers at both public and private agencies. It has a "reputation"; having failed repeatedly, it is labeled impossible and hopeless.

For its part, this family typically distrusts the "helping profession." Despite years of involvement with the social service system, it has not obtained the help it wants; worse, its problems may have been compounded by the system. The cadre involved with the family may eventually have replicated the patterns and conflicts in the family, becoming disorganized and discouraged, mirroring or recreating the family's confusion.

Repeated negative interactions have contributed to a pervasive atmosphere of negativity in which both the family and the worker have lost hope. The worker may have tried to impose her values and goals on the family and does not understand why the family is not motivated to change. The family is frustrated and despairing. Eventually the relationship between the worker and the multineed family is characterized by mutual alienation or even hostility. Then a process of mutual withdrawal occurs between the family and society. Society and its institutions withdraw assistance from the family or become increasingly punitive since the family appears unresponsive. The problem for the family now becomes chronic.

Given their history with the social service system, families are highly skeptical about trusting yet another new worker. And why shouldn't they be? When a family brings up its negative history with previous workers, it is imperative the new worker acknowledge what the family is saying. It's important to let the family know that they would be crazy to trust a new worker after what they have been through. The only way for them to be sure that they can trust someone new is to see if, over time, this new worker can actually assist them. New workers should never promise anything they, themselves, cannot personally deliver or guarantee, especially if it involves other service systems. The family doesn't need another disappointment or failure. It takes time to disrupt the cycle of chronicity between a family and worker and to build a positive, trusting relationship.

Reentering Treatment: Failure or Strength?

It is time we recognized that a double standard exists for high-risk families, for two reasons. First, many do not have access to private services because they cannot afford them. Second, it is considered perfectly acceptable for a family who is perceived of as healthy to go into treatment to work on a particular issue and then return a few years later for assistance on the same or another issue. But when a high-risk family reenters treatment, it's judged a treatment failure.[13] Many family preservation programs even assess treatment efficacy based on whether a family returns to the program, which should never be the case. Why should anyone be penalized for seeking treatment? A program's goal is to give a family the best experience they've had with the "system" so that they'll seek future services more quickly.

If we spent more time "tuning up" families, we would spend less money on them in the long run. Car maintenance is a good analogy: The more preventive work you do (e.g., regularly changing the oil), the greater is the likelihood that your car will run well, last longer, and not require expensive major repairs. It is unfair of society to look down on families who seek services more than once. We should instead view this as a strength: Families have identified certain needs and have requested assistance to help resolve their problems before they become severe.

4
A Framework for Beginning Family Work

Those who work with high-risk families have to be careful about imposing their own values and beliefs on them. It is too easy to ask these families judgmental questions:

"Why aren't people making changes in their lives?"

"Why are they saying it won't work before they even try?"

"Why do parents smoke when they don't have enough money to put food on the table?"

"Why don't parents spend time playing with and enjoying their children?"

"Why does this single mother, on Aid to Families with Dependent Children for years, buy herself a dress instead of paying the electric bill?"

Let's look at this last question. This social worker is astounded because she would *never* make such a decision. This value judgment, however, fails to help the worker understand why the choice was made. Many multineed families have lived such a deprived existence for so long that buying clothes, a television set, or anything else gives them at least immediate gratification and offers temporary escape from reality. These families have lost hope of ever catching up with their bills. The decision not to pay one month's electric bill can't, from their point of view, make much difference in the scheme of things. In addition, many of these families are caught in a generational cycle: This is the way their parents lived, and they never learned to live any other way. They're not afraid of having their electricity or their telephone shut off; this has happened to them many times before. This is the way they live.

Similarly, the question about why parents do not play with their children stems from a value that places great importance on exposing children to a variety of diverse environments that stimulate and educate them. Parents in many high-risk families typically do not do this; their children often watch television at long length and play among themselves. Perhaps the mother is a single parent who has just become sober, and she lives with her four young children in a two-bedroom apartment. This woman works sixty hours a week sewing shirts at a factory. On weekends, she just wants to relax, yet her children argue among each other, and eventually she starts yelling at them. Certainly it would be valuable for this family to get out of their small apartment, yet this is not the mother's priority. She's overwhelmed and simply wants to recover from working hard all week. If a worker repeatedly tries to persuade the mother that this is a priority, the mother will most likely ignore the worker. For her, other issues are much more pressing. The worker must keep in mind that if the family doesn't consider an idea priority, it's irrelevant that the worker thinks it's important.

The assumptions workers make about families drive the questions they ask and determine the interventions chosen. Since assumptions drive our work, we must be clear about our assumptions. We come to our job with a set of values and beliefs. If, while working with a family, we make value judgments, implying that our values are better than a family's, we are sure to fail. We may not agree with a family's values, but we do need to respect the family.

Focusing on the Family

When a high-risk family is referred to a family preservation program, they often come with a thick file. It is wise not to read the case file before first meeting the family or you may never want to see them. Most files are very negative and create an adverse framework from which to begin treatment. It is better to meet with the family, form impressions without any preconceived notions, and then read the case file.

Too often we ignore or only superficially involve the family, or we say we do family work yet work only with individual family members. Each family, however, is composed of an interlocking web of relationships. When one family member has a problem, it affects the entire family. Although the family will most likely be referred for a problem with a single member, the worker must conceptualize the family unit as the client. The family typically expects the worker to "fix" the person who has been identified as the "problem" and usually expects to have minimal involvement in the process. The worker's task is to broaden the focus, helping the family recognize and acknowledge that all family members contribute, knowingly or unknowingly, to the maintenance of the identified client's symptom. Family members can contribute to the solution; by working together they can change their situation.

Understanding systems theory and terminology is useful in both assessment and treatment. Salvador Munuchin's *Families and Family Therapy* is highly recommended; it explains structural family therapy and presents a systems vocabulary that enables workers to see beyond the individual. Maintaining "a 'family focus' does not always mean seeing the family together, but does imply considering the systemic effect of all issues, including therapeutic interventions."[1] It may be that the worker will never see the entire family (defined as the immediate and extended family as well as significant others) together, but will need to maintain a systems approach that recognizes the importance of all members, even those who are absent (e.g., a parent who is incarcerated, a parent who has deserted the family, a parent who has died, a parent who refuses to participate in family meetings). Individual, couples, or group counseling is provided when and if it contributes to family functioning.

Assessing Family Needs in Partnership with the Family

The process of uniting with a family by sharing common experiences is the key to successful treatment. "The important part of helping," says one author, "is the relationship."[2] Families need to know that this worker is going to stick by them over the long haul. Workers must show genuine respect for families as full participants in the treatment process. They must appreciate families' varied coping styles, believe that families have the capacity for change, and recognize and accentuate the strengths of each family member.

The focus of the assessment is on establishing a relationship with the family. Information gathering is important, but the process itself lays the groundwork for developing a partnership. The worker and family conduct a mutual assessment, identifying strengths and prioritizing areas of concern. The worker's job is to join the family where *they* are, not where the worker wants them to be. The more involved the family is in verbalizing and prioritizing their needs, the greater is the likelihood that they will be committed to change. "No matter how skilled the worker, little enduring change will occur if the goals of treatment are not the family's."[3] Sometimes parents expect the worker to be the expert and want to turn over all responsibility; workers who acquiesce and set goals for the family will fail in reaching their goal.

Assessment is not a separate and distinct process, but an ongoing process, necessitating continual reevaluation and requiring a systemic understanding of family functioning. It uses tools designed to respond to the unique needs of each family and incorporates culturally sensitive techniques (see Chapter 7). The initial assessment involves the whole family and, if possible, the extended family, foster parents, and significant others.

Assessment Tools

Assessment tools designed to encourage total family participation are recommended. In addition to providing the family and worker with information, they are a nonthreatening and an engaging means by which to involve the family.

The *genogram* is a nonthreatening, interactive way of involving the family in considering the complexity of family roles, patterns, and relationships that have evolved over generations. It gives the worker and family members an understanding of the family's history and may reveal important information to family members. The goal of using a genogram is to determine what generational themes are present and how these affect the family.

The *ecomap*, another useful tool, helps families conceptualize their relationships with other systems, indicating sources of support and stress. Constructing an ecomap helps to determine how the interplay between the family and the environment affects the family. Families often find the process of drawing an ecomap useful because it is visual and concrete. Using this tool may alleviate a family's anxiety because it takes the focus off internal family problems, acknowledging and emphasizing the overlap between the family and their environment.

It is optimal to encourage the family to glean their own interpretations from the genogram and the ecomap. The worker may then put forth tentative hypotheses, continually asking the family for feedback. When offering hypotheses, it is important to mention strengths first, then concerns.[4]

Just as we consider individual stages of development, so must we assess the family within the context of a developmental framework. Thus, the worker examines the ability of family members to negotiate key developmental stages during the life cycle and make an assessment along a continuum. This exercise is useful for the family because they learn that every family goes through individual and family stages of development but adjusts to each stage differently. If the worker can frame any problems as developmental issues, the family may be relieved to conceptualize the problem from this perspective instead of thinking there is something inherently wrong with them.[5]

Another visual, concrete, and tangible assessment tool is a timeline, which highlights prominent family events along a vertical line. The family's identification of key events and their dates and brief descriptions enable the worker and family members to see what life events they consider salient. A timeline is a self-assessment vehicle that demonstrates to the family how they have responded to positive and negative events in their lives. It clarifies areas in which family members possess strengths and reveals areas in which they need improvement.

The behavior sequence chart, yet another assessment tool, offers a circular, rather than linear, interpretation of behavior. Linear thinking considers only cause and effect; circular thinking examines the context of the behavior, how everyone is involved in the problem, consequences of the behavior, why the behavior is maintained, and how it is reinforced. Once a behavior sequence has been diagrammed, the worker can consider various points of intervention. There is no "right" place to intervene; the worker can intervene at one of any number of places. The behavior sequence chart expands intervention options. It also teaches families to think systemically and recognize how each family member's behavior affects the problem and potentially the solution.

Assessment Report

A written assessment report includes the following information:

- Determination of concrete needs.
- Recognition of health, medical, and dental needs.
- Identification of disabilities.
- Identification of family strengths and resources, including previous successes and accomplishments, problem-solving skills, and coping skills.
- Identification of family difficulties.
- Previous attempts at alleviating problems.
- An intergenerational family history.
- Information about the family's culture (e.g., strengths and barriers regarding problem resolution, the need for resources relevant to the family's culture).
- Identification of internal family dynamics.
- Risk assessment for child abuse (physical and sexual) and neglect, as well as domestic violence.
- Substance abuse assessment.
- Identification of informal and formal supports that are currently supportive, those that have the potential for being positive, and those that are problematic.
- Determination of the treatment goals of family members.

Family-based assessments work from a growth development model, not a medical model. The goal is not to come up with diagnoses or labels for family members. Workers should not write anything in their assessments (or any other reports for that matter) that they would not feel comfortable having a family read. In fact, the worker encourages the family to read all reports, as well as letters to agencies and the court. This puts them in control as an active participant.

Families fully collaborate with the worker in developing their own treatment plan, which is based on the assessment. It identifies treatment goals, behavioral objectives to achieve these goals, interventions to meet the objectives, identification of who is responsible for the specified interventions, and time frames. Goals are realistically attainable; stated in tangible, measurable, behavioral terms; and salient to the client. They are defined in small steps that are achievable to minimize the possibility of failure. Measurable behavioral objectives are used to let the worker and the family know that change has occurred. If goals are not being achieved, the worker and family reevaluate the assessment. The treatment plan is reviewed and updated regularly.

Reframing Needs: A Positive Perspective

Perception determines attitude in family-based work. Instead of perceiving a family as failing, for example, a worker should conceptualize family members as treading water and struggling to keep their heads above water. Their way of life demands considerable energy. Instead of penalizing and denigrating families for their failures, we must give them credit for struggling to keep their lives together.

The presenting problem may or may not have something to do with what the family wants. The first step is to listen to the family, acknowledge what they are saying, and help them figure out their goals. Then the problem is defined in a way that it can be solved. This entails shifting from a pathology-centered to a possibility-focused, goal-oriented, and solution-focused approach. Measurable and realistic goals are developed. For example, asking a parent to spend quality time with a child is neither measurable nor realistic. However, asking a parent to do a puzzle or play a game with the child twice each week is both specific and achievable.

Assessments then, are structured to give families hope. Problems are conceptualized as skill deficits to avoid blame, expand treatment alternatives, and offer hope for change. It is easier to increase a skill than stop a negative behavior. Treatment options are generated when an assessment expands rather than limits alternatives. For example, "Mrs. Lambert will find alternative ways to discipline her children" is easier to work on than "Mrs. Lambert will stop yelling at her children." The first assessment opens up a number of possibilities for intervention, such as participation in a parent support group, obtaining behavior management tools, or attending parent effectiveness training.

First Encounters

Families with a long history of involvement with the social service system and well-intentioned but misguided workers are often, not surprisingly, defensive and angry when they realize they must become involved with it again. It has repeatedly let them down and sometimes even contributed to their problems. Since they often haven't had a positive experience in the past, they expect the worst.

The worker confronted with this situation acknowledges this history and regards the family's response as healthy. His first task is to establish a relationship and partnership with the family to enable them to take control of their own lives. As a relationship develops, the family may continue to be ambivalent as the members try to decide whether they can trust the counselor. The counselor could characterize this attitude as resistance—or as healthy skepticism. His determination changes the whole dynamic. The counselor's attitude is essential to work successfully with families. A family who *expects* the worker to be just like previous workers will be surprised when he is different, patiently moving at the family's pace, rather than his own, or the preconceived pace of some model to which he must adhere.

Effective workers search out, reinforce, and amplify whatever strengths the family has. (Anyone can find pathology; it's more challenging to discern strengths.) People are more motivated to change when their strengths are acknowledged and supported than when their limitations are repeatedly discussed. A family asked to identify strengths they've used in the past to get through difficult times may be surprised at the worker's focus on what they have done right, and typically they are responsive. This helps lower the family's reluctance and assists in developing a partnership.

Resistance is always a possibility; it can take many forms and be expressed directly or indirectly. Direct resistance in the form of outright hostility is easier to deal with because it is out in the open. Indirect resistance is less identifiable; it includes missing or being late for appointments, agreeing with everything the worker says, or responding laconically to questions. For example, Steve was on his way to visit a family that had just been referred. He knocked on their door; no one answered. He waited a few minutes and knocked again. Still no answer. But Steve was persistent, and after ten minutes or so Mr. Carter opened the door. Before Steve could introduce himself, Mr. Carter said, "I hate goddamn social workers; they're all the same!" and slammed the door. Steve sat on the porch for fifteen minutes, then left the family a note. He acknowledged Mr. Carter's anger toward social workers based on past experience and expressed an interest in hearing more about it, asking for just one opportunity to hear the family's point of view. He said he would return the following week, on the same day and at the same time, and he hoped the family would talk with him.

The following week Steve was back. He knocked on the door and again received no response. As he waited, he could hear a baby crying inside the house, but no one opened the door. He wrote the family a second note, not much different from the first. When Steve returned the following week, Mr. Carter opened the door, exclaiming, "No one in my family believes that you could be so stupid as to keep coming back here when we won't even open the door for you. I'll give you just a few minutes. Come in."

Although the family let Steve in the house, he realized this was just the first step. He had gotten inside; now he needed to figure out how to stay there. Steve went on to successfully work with this family.

5
Treatment Strategies

The Fitzgerald family was made up of Mrs. Fitzgerald, age fifty; her live-in boyfriend, Joel, age sixty-three; and her four children from two former marriages: Nancy, age twenty-five; Susan, age twenty-three; Dennis, age fifteen; and Bob, age nine. Her oldest daughter was married and lived away from home. Dennis who was under the auspices of the state juvenile justice agency and living in a residential program, had been picked up for breaking and entering on a number of occasions, and he had a history of car theft. In addition, he was a behavior problem in school and had low grades.

The family was referred to a family-based program when Dennis was about to return home. Nancy, the family-based counselor, had visited Mrs. Fitzgerald at her home a few weeks prior to Dennis's return. While they chatted over tea, Mrs. Fitzgerald said that she was tired of having young social workers visit her, ask a lot of questions, write down everything she said, and then leave. Nevertheless, as they talked at some length, they started to get to know each other. Mrs. Fitzgerald talked about her children, especially Dennis, and their conversation turned to Dennis's return home and what the family thought it would need to make it successful. During this visit, Bob tromped through the kitchen and was introduced to Nancy, and later Joel came home from work and was introduced also. Mrs. Fitzgerald and Nancy made an appointment to meet two days later.

Their next meeting too consisted of conversation over tea. Nancy asked how she could be of assistance, but Mrs. Fitzgerald said she had no clue. Anyway, wasn't the program supposed to help her son? He had the problem, after all.

Nancy continued to visit the Fitzgerald family, two to three times a week, spending one to three hours each visit. She was always nonjudgmental, inquisitive, and interested. After a month or so, Nancy and Mrs. Fitzgerald had clearly established a relationship characterized by mutual respect and trust. Nancy learned about Mrs. Fitzgerald's Portuguese grandmother, who, with her father, had raised her because her mother had disappeared. They talked at length about Mrs. Fitzgerald's and Joel's families of origin. Mrs. Fitzgerald began to look forward to the meetings, frequently calling Nancy at her office to see when she would come next. If Mrs. Fitzgerald felt the need to talk, she knew Nancy would try to stop by or that at least she could talk to Nancy on the telephone. Nancy was flexible; if she could change her schedule, she would. For her part, Nancy was gratified that Mrs. Fitzgerald felt comfortable enough to initiate a meeting.

When Dennis came for a home visit with his residential counselor, both Nancy and the counselor joined Mrs. Fitzgerald and Dennis for lunch. They talked about what Dennis's mother expected of him when he came home, as well as other concerns she had. Dennis too had concerns about returning home, which they discussed as well. It was agreed that a family meeting would be held later in the week to discuss Dennis's homecoming.

All family members living at home except Joel, took part in the family meeting, along with Nancy and Dennis's counselor. Dennis talked about how he had learned to follow rules in residential treatment, and he hoped he could improve his behavior at home and at school. The family discussed Dennis's curfew. Mrs. Fitzgerald said that in the past she had ignored Dennis's complaints, refusing to listen to him. She hoped to be a better listener now and agreed to discuss any rules with Dennis if he considered them to be unfair. She also promised to work on setting consistent limits, something she had difficulty doing. It was agreed that Dennis would come home in two weeks and enroll in an alternative high school.

Weekly family meetings were held once Dennis returned home. Although Joel was always invited, he didn't show an interest in attending. Mrs. Fitzgerald, Dennis, Susan, and Bob were always there. The children looked forward to Nancy's visits just as much as their mother did, for they too had established a strong bond with her. During these meetings, the family learned how to communicate with each other. They realized that they hadn't listened to each other in the past and had rarely given each other positive feedback.

Then two months after returning home, Dennis was again arrested for car theft. When Mrs. Fitzgerald called Nancy at home and asked if they could meet at the police station, Nancy readily agreed. Dennis was released to his mother's custody and went home. Nancy attended his arraignment the next morning in a room on the second floor of the courthouse. Mrs. Fitzgerald was not there; she was acrophobic and refused to leave the ground floor. Immediately following the arraignment, a juvenile justice agency caseworker asked for a meeting. Nancy arranged for them to meet in a first-floor conference room so that Mrs. Fitzgerald could participate. The purpose of the conference was to determine whether Dennis could remain at home or if he needed to return to the residential program. Dennis wanted to stay home, and Mrs. Fitzgerald and Nancy supported him. Mrs. Fitzgerald's response was very different from her previous responses when Dennis got in trouble.

She hoped Dennis could remain at home and continue work with the family-based program.

The caseworker was surprised to see Mrs. Fitzgerald because she had never before come to a meeting; rather, the caseworker had always gone to her house. He had assumed Mrs. Fitzgerald was disinterested, when in reality it was her fear of heights that kept her away. In fact, all of the many people who had worked with Mrs. Fitzgerald in the past had failed to get her to attend any meeting regarding her son, possibly because they were unaware of her phobia.

As Mrs. Fitzgerald's commitment to the family-based program grew, Nancy arranged for other mothers in similar circumstances to form a parent support group. Since Mrs. Fitzgerald felt most comfortable in her home, it was decided that everyone would meet there. Nancy picked up two of the mothers, and one mother drove there alone. Over coffee and doughnuts, the women shared stories of their children's involvement with the juvenile justice system. They got along well and decided to meet monthly to work on crafts and talk. Mrs. Fitzgerald was very creative and agreed to teach everyone, including Nancy, how to make latch hook rugs. Everyone purchased a kit, and this group of five began meeting regularly. Whenever Nancy made home visits, she brought along her rug, and Mrs. Fitzgerald helped Nancy while they discussed issues concerning Mrs. Fitzgerald's family, coming up with possible solutions.

Nancy's supervisor, David, was an experienced family therapist and from time to time accompanied Nancy on family visits as a regular part of her supervision. When Mrs. Fitzgerald first met David, she immediately took a liking to him, and as time went on the Fitzgeralds developed a relationship with him as well. He was unassuming, funny, told jokes, and created an informal environment in which the family felt comfortable. Nancy and David's sincere caring and concern were evident to the family. Finally, after hearing so much about Nancy's supervisor, even Joel decided to participate in one of the family meetings with Nancy and David.

The parent support group continued to meet once a month, and the mothers called each other between meetings. Sometimes the women got together to play bingo or bowl. Most were single parents and welcomed the opportunity to get out with friends.

The commissioner of the state juvenile justice agency became aware of the support group and asked if he could meet these mothers. They agreed and Mrs. Fitzgerald offered to have the meeting in her home. Since Mrs. Fitzgerald thought that her house wasn't in the best condition, she asked her family and program staff to join together to clean and paint to get ready for this visit. The Fitzgeralds and program staff painted the living room, cleaned the dining room, and hung curtains. The commissioner visited, accompanied by a reporter, and listened as the women talked about what the program had enabled them to do, how much they liked getting together, and how the program had affected their families.

Nancy continued to work with the Fitzgerald family for almost eighteen months. Dennis continued to attend school regularly and obtained a part-time job. Over that time, Mrs. Fitzgerald's relationship with Dennis improved dramatically, and she became a spokesperson for the program, talking to state officials and attending meetings regardless of whether they were held on the ground floor. When Nancy terminated her work with the family, Mrs. Fitzgerald gave Nancy a hand-knitted sweater to express her gratitude for all that Nancy had done. Nancy and Mrs. Fitzgerald unquestionably had a relationship characterized by reciprocity. Mrs. Fitzgerald gave something to Nancy in exchange for her help, and she also gave something back to the community when she became a spokesperson for the program. The program terminated with the Fitzgerald family but Nancy continued to stay in touch. Mrs. Fitzgerald accompanied Nancy on home visits to families new to the program so that they could meet someone who had made significant life changes.

When the program decided to increase its staff, Nancy suggested to Mrs. Fitzgerald that she apply for a position. Mrs. Fitzgerald was hired by the same program in which she had been a client. She worked every day in her office on the fourth floor of a six-story building. She had truly been empowered.

The concept of empowerment is the cornerstone of all family-based programs. Empowerment encompasses a way of thinking about families. It's a conviction that families deserve respect, have strengths, *can* make changes in their lives, and are resilient, and it means helping families gain *access* to their power, not giving them power. A clear understanding, commitment, and belief in this mind-set is essential. The worker must believe in the family and communicate that she knows they are capable of getting their needs met and handling their own difficulties. This approach to treatment is a nontraditional way of thinking about and working with families, and it requires operating under a new set of assumptions and rules.

The worker assumes a pragmatic approach—down-to-earth, practical, hands-on, and nonideological—that is designed to work with each family individually. Creativity, flexibility, and the use of multidimensional interventions play a role in work with multiple-need families. There is a great deal of variation among families in regard to their strengths, coping styles, difficulties, ability to advocate for themselves, cultural and ethnic connections, sexual preference, and access to formal and informal supports. Thus, service delivery must be highly individualized.

The worker's role is to act as facilitator, advocate, and ally. Family members may not believe they are capable of meeting their own needs, so the worker's job is to convey a genuine belief in the family and be available when the family needs support. The worker helps the family believe in itself, instilling pride, courage, self-esteem, and hope for the future.

The worker does not tell a family what areas they need to work on; rather, the worker and family problem-solve collaboratively, with the worker following the family's lead, moving at their pace. A worker who tries to prioritize a family's needs and dictate treatment goals gives the family a negative message, disempowering them by telling them that they are incapable of dealing with their problems. In this new model, the worker no longer serves as an expert but as a collaborator and facilitator.

Workers empower families in six ways:

1. Believing in their ability to change and helping families believe in themselves.

2. Providing families with a new perspective or outlook.

3. Educating families and helping them increase their own skills.

4. Recognizing and building on therapeutically useful strengths and resources.

5. Helping families realize that they do have alternatives and options.

6. Designing intervention strategies that support and strengthen families' cultural and ethnic backgrounds.

Empowerment is the underlying theme of family-based programs that the worker reinforces in all aspects of assessment and treatment. The overarching goal of family preservation is to strengthen families' coping skills and improve their ability to function effectively in the community. The rest of this chapter looks at general strategies.

Addressing Concrete Needs

Assessing and responding to a family's immediate concrete needs is the worker's first priority.[1] Families often report that this assistance is the most useful service they received.[2] Assisting with concrete needs is of paramount importance in effecting change and offers a vehicle through which to establish a partnership and trusting relationship before moving on to psychological issues. Families tend to respond positively to this initial help for three reasons: they may distrust workers based on past experience, they may not respond well to "talk therapy," and for many, English is a second language, necessitating concrete assistance in such tasks as completing applications and negotiating social service bureaucracies.

Concrete needs encompass a range of services: helping a family obtain housing, providing transportation, finding day care, or setting up a budget. These activities provide the foundation for the development of a trusting relationship between worker and family. Moreover, these basic needs must be addressed before families can be motivated to look at psychological needs, such as developing a loving, caring relationship with one's children.[3] For example, a mother who is unable to make her food stamps last because she has no transportation to reach a grocery store and is forced to pay higher prices at a corner store within walking distance will be so preoccupied with this basic human need that a note from her daughter's teacher saying that her daughter is not handing in her homework may seem trivial in comparison. This mother is worried about her daughter's having enough food to eat. Part of the daughter's problem may be that she is hungry and can't concentrate on her schoolwork in the evening. The simple solution of transportation to the grocery store would be a significant intervention.

A number of family-based programs set aside flexible funds to purchase items families need but cannot afford. A typical amount to set aside is $100 to $500 per family to be used to buy a bed, repair a car, buy a washing machine, or other important items. Programs that have flexible funds are recognizing the relationship between concrete needs and emotional well-being.

Dealing with concrete needs first is also less intimidating for families than addressing psychological issues. They view concrete needs as external, impersonal, separate from themselves, and unconnected to their self-worth. A family that doesn't have enough food or has had its electricity shut off does not believe that these problems mean there is something intrinsically wrong with them, and since these are not personal issues, the family tends to be more open to letting a worker assist in finding a solution. Addressing concrete needs proves to a family that the worker can do something for them besides offer talk therapy. Additionally, research studies have determined that effective counseling addresses concrete as well as psychological needs.[4]

Sometimes family members expect to fail even at concrete tasks. Therefore, small tasks should be tackled first to ensure success. Setting small goals makes a task manageable and creates an atmosphere in which success is virtually ensured, so a despairing family member is not once again faced with failure. The more successes a client has, no matter how small, the more the client's self-esteem improves, confidence increases, and belief in his or her ability to negotiate problems develops. Repeated success encourages clients to have hope and confidence in themselves and in their ability to make changes, and it instills in them the belief that their situation can change. Consider the analogy of a child learning how to ride a bicycle. We begin by teaching the child to ride the bicycle with training wheels, urging the child on and cheering at the child's successes. Eventually that child learns how to ride alone. The teaching has progressed one step at a time, at the child's pace. The same is true of working with multineed families.

A family that has successfully coped with concrete day-to-day concerns feels accomplished and motivated to move on to deal with more difficult and complex problems. This process also encourages the family's trust in the worker and a belief that the worker can assist in tackling complicated issues.

For example, when a worker was making a second home visit, the parents mentioned that they wanted to clear a space in the backyard for their two children to play. The worker offered to help and they agreed when to begin. The worker, parents, and children first cleared brush and trash from the yard of the apartment building. Next, they planted some grass seed; all felt a sense of accomplishment when the grass began to grow. Next, they built a sandbox, and the worker solicited some donated toys for the children. The participation between the worker and family altered the negative impression the family had of professional helpers and enabled the worker to observe how the family members related to each other while accomplishing a task.

Some counselors, especially those new to the field, may feel overwhelmed or even intimidated by families that have so many needs. By initially focusing on concrete needs, the worker, like the family members, will feel accomplished with the small successes. Meeting concrete needs serves as the foundation for a successful worker-family partnership.

Developing a Model Relationship and Partnership

A number of studies have identified the counselor-family relationship as the key element in provision of effective service delivery.[5] Although establishing a relationship may seem to be an easy task to a counselor trained in human relations, it is often difficult to accomplish, especially if the family has a negative history of involvement with the social service system.

Developing a relationship with a family may have more to do with the family's history and opinion of the helping profession than it does with the skills of the worker. Perhaps the family has been labeled as difficult, hard to reach, and resistant to treatment by the many workers and agencies with whom they have been involved previously. Their poor experiences in the past, which may have resulted in the removal of a child, give them no reason to trust a new worker or believe that she can help. One way to overcome the family's negative stereotype is to listen as family members reveal their prior experiences, describe their needs, and tell the worker the help they need. A worker who takes this approach communicates respect for the family.

Assisting in meeting concrete needs helps family members begin to trust the worker and believe that she is truly there to help. Sometimes being a presence for the family through a stressful time can be helpful. A bond can be established if the worker is willing to spend time with the family in their home, perhaps sitting in the kitchen drinking tea or coffee, having a conversation. This is time well spent in establishing a relationship that will grow into a partnership.

The worker's goal, to become a trusted, accepting partner, is furthered as the counselor acts as nurturer, teacher, role model, advocate, and facilitator. The focus of the relationship is on problem solving, decision making, coping, and building on strengths. Family members develop the capacity for collaboration and negotiation through the context of a meaningful, caring relationship characterized by mutual respect. By empowering the family to become independent, able to meet its own needs, the worker prepares them for the time when they will be on their own. The worker teaches them to recognize and rely on their own inner resources and how to use the resources in the community. The worker is thus in charge of the process; the family is in charge of the outcome. The following example illustrates how this approach works.

While visiting Dorothy, the worker commented on an artificial flower arrangement on the kitchen table. Dorothy said she had made it and when the worker said she'd like one for her desk at work, Dorothy promptly offered to teach her. They went shopping at the local mall to get the materials and then stopped for lunch. On her next visit, Dorothy showed the worker how to put the flower arrangement together. Several colleagues at work admired the arrangement and asked the counselor where she had purchased the flowers. When she told them that she had made the arrangement with the help of one of her clients, they asked whether Dorothy would help them too. Dorothy was delighted to give a flower arranging class to the staff, who suggested to her that she might be able to sell some arrangements.

The worker encourages family members to participate in treatment so they do not feel as if it is "something that is happening to them"—a not uncommon perception since professionals have a history of setting priorities for families, coordinating treatment, and judging compliance, all the while excluding the family from the discussion. To build a family's trust, the worker can show the family their file. Sharing the file reinforces trust, proving to the family that the worker is working with them, not reporting on them. Families can have ready access to their files and even write reports and develop service plans.

To develop a successful partnership and model relationship, the worker is both genuine and respectful. Nevertheless, "there is a balance between genuine . . . concern and maintaining distance that is difficult to define and more difficult to achieve."[6] Creating clear boundaries is crucial for both the family and the worker. Unless a worker maintains objectivity, both worker and family suffer.

The worker can become a role model by sharing personal information, especially relating to resolving a particular problem. Sharing an experience or giving examples of others in the same situation as family members is important. Families may forget the discussion itself, but they rarely forget the experiences the worker described that gave them hope. This principle is illustrated by the following example.

Mr. and Mrs. Alvarez were quite upset by a note from their daughter's teacher. It seems that their daughter, Christina, would rather talk and giggle with her friends than pay attention in class, and the Alvarezes were not sure what to do. The worker then shared his own experience, describing how his son had had a similar problem of inattention. He had dealt with it by letting his son stay up late one night each week to watch his favorite television show if the teacher reported the boy was doing well. Otherwise he had to go to bed at his usual bedtime. The worker went on to discuss the concept of rewarding good behavior instead of punishing bad behavior. The worker's discussion encouraged the Alvarezes to come up with a similar plan for Christina. Later, when they were asked how they fostered their daughter's change in behavior, they did not remember the concept the worker had explained, but they clearly recalled the experience the worker had shared with them.

A true partnership is established when there is reciprocity. The worker provides help to the family as well as accepting help from the family. For example, a worker moving into a new apartment was having difficulty getting a truck and finding people to help with the move. One of the families she was working with offered the use of their truck, and family members volunteered to help. The worker accepted the family's assistance and cooked a spaghetti dinner for everyone after the move to show her thanks. The reciprocity made the relationship between the worker and family more equitable.

Finally, an important part of any relationship is having fun. Many high-risk families are so caught up in a quagmire of despair and crisis that they have forgotten how to have a good time—or perhaps they never learned. A number of activities can be done at little expense: a family walk in the park, card or board games, singing together, or reading a story, for example. The worker helps the family find ways to enjoy themselves and helps them recognize the importance of fun.

Reparenting

Once a model relationship based on trust has developed between the family and worker, the next step is reparenting: that is, the worker provides the nurturing that many parents failed to receive from their own parents, offering consistency, support, and hope. "Through their relationship with the worker, parents find someone that they can depend on, decreasing their need to depend upon their own children in unhealthy and inappropriate ways."[7] The counselor focuses on the parents now because changes in family dynamics are reinforced by parents.

The relationship between worker and parents serves as a model. Many high-risk parents received little nurturing as children; in addition, they often have no positive parenting role models and possess a limited knowledge of child development. Nurturing the parents and helping them develop self-confidence benefits their children. Before they can "respond effectively and positively to their children, their own needs must be met."[8] Parents with substance abuse problems, no job, no place to live, little to eat, or conflictual relationships are unable to nurture their children. Once parents begin to deal with their own problems, develop self-confidence, and obtain some small successes, they can be more responsive to their children.[9]

During a weekly support group for single mothers, the worker asked the mothers how they had been disciplined by their own parents when they were children. Most said they had been yelled at and spanked, sometimes severely, and they recalled how they felt unloved and bad when they were punished in these ways. The discussion then focused on how these mothers would like to treat their children. All said they wanted to be better parents to their children than their parents had been to them. They wanted to learn and use less severe discipline and wanted their children to know they were loved.

Putting Parents in Charge

The family should actively participate in determining treatment goals. When the worker puts parents in charge, he is conveying to the entire family a belief in the parents' competence. The message is that he believes the parents love their children and want to do what is best for them. If given viable choices, almost all parents will choose a course of action that will not harm their children.[10]

Many parents think only in terms of good and bad behavior, not in terms of values. A worker should help parents conceptualize their values and determine how they can structure their family life to reflect them. (Workers must be careful not to inject their own values during this process.) Once parents recognize which values are important to them, they can determine the rules the family needs to follow and what the consequences will be if these rules are broken. Perhaps they can list the values and then come up with rules to match each one. This exercise gives parents practical ways to translate values into rules in an effort to transmit these values to their children.

A single mother was distressed that her nine-year-old son and seven-year-old daughter were extremely disrespectful to adults, using back-talk and even profanity. The mother had been brought up by *her* mother to treat others, especially her elders, with respect. Once the mother recognized that she considered respect an important value, she asked for help in finding a way to change her children's behavior. She first explained to her children why respect was important to her. Then she created a family rule—the children were to respond to adults in a respectful manner, which meant being polite and not using profanity—and a consequence of breaking the rule—the children would not be able to invite friends to play after dinner. Although she needed much support from the worker to enforce the rule consistently, this mother was finally able to do it on her own. Her success in changing her children's behavior empowered her.

Parents are put in charge when they are supported by their worker during family meetings. These meetings, attended by all members, offer an opportunity for each member to discuss and suggest ways to resolve their own problems as well as those of other family members. Initially they should occur weekly; as the family learns to resolve issues on their own, meetings can diminish in frequency (although a family member may call an emergency meeting for help in resolving a pressing problem). Many families continue to hold family meetings on their own after they have terminated with their counselor.

During a family meeting, a contract may be written clearly outlining the responsibilities of each family member. This contract is monitored and discussed at subsequent meetings. Teenagers respond positively to this tool because it opens lines of communication, and they usually get something in return for agreeing to adhere to the contract. A contract also serves as a benchmark to measure changes taking place within the family.

Mr. and Mrs. Moser and their two sons, fifteen-year-old Tom and twelve-year-old Martin, were involved in a family-based counseling program. At the suggestion of their counselor, they decided to hold family meetings. First, the worker and family established ground rules: no verbal or physical abuse, only one person talking at a time, and no one leaves the meeting until it's over. Then they moved on to the issue of the boys' helping around the house since both parents worked full time. Mrs. Moser thought it would be helpful if they cleaned their rooms, did the dishes after dinner, regularly took out the trash, and stopped fighting with each other. The boys said they were willing—*if* they got an allowance for the work. Their father pointed out that they were part of the family and should help in return for having a house to live in and food on the table. As they debated the matter, the parents were able to convince their sons to do the chores without an allowance, but they offered to extend their curfews one weekend night. At the worker's suggestion, they put this agreement in writing, drawing up a contract listing the chores and the new privileges, which each family member signed. It was placed on the refrigerator so that everyone could refer to it during the week. A meeting was scheduled for the following week to review the contract and revise it, if necessary, and to determine the agenda for the next family meeting.

Highly stressed parents may view themselves as ineffectual in dealing with their children's acting-out behavior and consider this just one more area in which they have failed. The worker can help parents to find ways to reduce their irritability, teaching them to view their child's behavior problem as a "technical difficulty" instead of personalizing it and becoming reactive. Working with parents to come up with specific ways to regain control is key. Sometimes it means helping parents realize that there are a number of ways to handle a situation. A child, for example, may act out; the parents then yell at the child. In response, the child acts out more, and the parents yell louder.

These parents are paralyzed; their response clearly isn't working but they nevertheless continue to use it. The worker helps these parents recognize this pattern and determine possible alternatives.

An example of putting parents in charge is illustrated by Tina, a hyperactive five-year-old who would not follow her parents' directions. After a family meeting with Tina's parents, one technique proved successful. The parents got Tina's attention by turning her face toward them, and telling her to put on her "listening ears." This enabled the parents to give Tina instructions.

A second example is illustrated by a father of four whose seven-year-old, Jonathan, routinely yelled and screamed at bedtime. Since all of the children shared a bedroom, this posed a problem. Long after the other children were asleep, Jonathan would get up to ask his father questions. Jonathan's father eventually became so frustrated that he beat Jonathan. Having been reported to a child protection agency by a neighbor who noticed Jonathan's bruises, the family was referred to a home-based family treatment program. Together the worker and father devised a plan to structure bedtime. Each night after dinner, Jonathan's father gave his son a bath and then read to all of the children. Jonathan then took his crayons and coloring book to bed and drew pictures or looked at or read a book until he got tired. Jonathan's father told his son to do this quietly. The next evening, he and his father discussed the pictures. Creating structure or rituals around bedtime is helpful.

Building on Strengths to Create Hope in Families

Historically, social service assessments have focused on family deficits, not on family capabilities. That is, traditional treatment consists of identifying what is wrong with people and then helping them to correct or accept those limitations or pathologies. We do families a serious injustice when we approach treatment from this perspective. Instead, we must shift to a growth-development model, looking "at what is right with families rather than always looking at their problems and deficiencies."[11] Every family has strengths and competencies; the worker's job "is to help people learn to recognize and appreciate their strengths and to believe in their capacities to develop, to help themselves, and to be independent."[12] The worker's focus is on shoring up and amplifying families' strengths and resources.

There is much talk about working from strengths, but little written on how to identify strengths and even less on professional training. Many workers consequently have no idea of how to go about doing it. The task begins by searching out the skills a family does have. A worker on a home visit needs to look around. Are there homemade pillows on the sofa? Is there a delicious aroma of home cooked food? Is there a vegetable garden? The worker's comments on the presence of these talents will contribute to the family's self-esteem and identify a subject for conversation.[13] People like to talk about what they feel good about and proud of. Taking an interest in what the family values is critical in establishing a relationship. A worker finds something about the family that she can respect and something about them that she likes.

A focus on building self-esteem discourages family resistance. People are more motivated to change when their strengths are supported. Instead of asking family members what their problems are, a worker can ask what strengths they bring to the family and what they think are the strengths of other family members. Individuals are often surprised to hear what others consider their strengths. Through this process, the worker helps the family discover its capabilities and formulate a new way to think about themselves. This approach facilitates treatment from a positive rather than negative framework, expanding the family's problem-solving options. The worker creates a language of strength, hope, and movement when talking with the family or about the family to other workers.[14]

Reframing and relabeling are ways to offer the family a different view of themselves. Reframing addresses a family theme (a pattern that maintains equilibrium in the family). The theme is acknowledged and discussed with the family, with the goal of having the family confront their view of themselves and then consider themselves in a new and different light. A counselor must carefully consider how to introduce a reframe to a family. Typically it is communicated in a tentative way and prefaced by statements such as, "It seems to me that . . . ," or "I get the impression that . . ." The goal is to present the reframe and encourage the family's feedback, all the while communicating concern for the family. A typical example of reframing is illustrated by a counselor who, in a family meeting, tells the parents, "Perhaps Kevin's acting out in school and his getting in trouble with the police is a valiant attempt on his part to keep the family together. I get the impression that Kevin's behavior provokes you, Mr. and Mrs. B., to communicate with each other because you're forced to deal with your son's getting in trouble. What do you think?"

Relabeling entails giving a new name to a pattern to change its value. Positively relabeling behaviors and statements that are perceived of as negative is a way to help the family recognize that what they consider deficits may actually be strengths. For example, a teenager may complain (as many do) that her parents nag about everything she does or wants to do or doesn't do. A worker relabels by stating that her parents must really care about her and must want to be sure that nothing bad happens to her. Relabeling can help the teenager recognize that her parents' "nagging" comes from caring. Once the adolescent understands and accepts this reasoning, she may be more willing to comply. As a result of the relabeling, the teenager and the parents feel better, and their relationship should improve.

Relabeling can serve to identify strengths. A mother who had no home for her two children and had to live in their car for a year may feel defeated. But the fact that they survived the ordeal and remained together is a strength, and the mother needs to view the experience from this perspective. Stimulating hope is the first step in developing the motivation to change.[15] Families are resilient; they can and have bounced back from innumerable negative experiences. If the mother in the example can consider herself a survivor of the experience and acknowledge her strength, she'll feel better about herself.

When people can identify strengths in one area of their lives, they can use them in other areas. For example, if a mother loses her temper and hits her child, the worker might want to explore how she responds in similar situations. Does she lose her temper at work? with friends? If she doesn't, the worker can help this mother figure out how she keeps cool at work and translate these strengths to her relationship with her child.

When looking for strengths, the worker must take the family's culture into consideration because what may be considered a strength in one culture may not be in another. In the European-American culture, individualism is valued and considered a strength. In many other cultures, including African-American, Hispanic, and Asian, identity is defined by one's family; the family, not the individual, is considered primary, and sacrificing individual needs for the family is viewed as a strength. A good example would be native Alaskan communities where group goals are more important than individual goals. In a group setting, a worker must be careful not to compliment an individual but instead compliment the group. In the home, family members are not encouraged to talk about themselves, and in community settings (such as a classroom), a child who is singled out and praised can feel ashamed. When working with a family, a worker emphasizes group goals and praises the entire family for improvement. In the village, everyone in the community is responsible for bringing up the children. It is a group effort, not just the effort of the parents.[16]

Frequent Contact and Availability

When working in a family-based program, the worker needs to be available at the family's convenience. This usually means on evenings and weekends. At the beginning of treatment, the worker may visit the family daily to support and get to know them. The length of the visit is mutually determined by the family and the worker. Frequent contact will give the worker valuable information and help build a partnership. It also gives the family the message that they are important and that the worker will give them the time they need. Frequent contact does not have to mean face-to-face meetings; telephone calls indicate to the family that the worker is regularly available to provide support, especially when difficult and painful problems occur; "they know that help and support are available whenever a crisis arises,"[17] typically at night or on the weekend, when most family members are home together and sharing space can generate tension.

Although a worker needs to be available for a crisis, it is imperative to set limits with the family. The worker and the family must reach some agreement about how to handle problems in the evenings and on weekends and how to know what constitutes a crisis that necessitates calling the worker, as opposed to the family's resolving the crisis on their own. If the worker is too readily available, jumping every time the family calls, the family gets the message that the worker does not believe that the family can handle its own problems. It's important for workers to maintain a balance between being available and being intrusive. Families may initially test a worker's boundaries, but they generally do not make inappropriate requests for crisis assistance.

That some multineed families do not have a telephone poses a different challenge. The worker and family can decide what steps to take in a crisis when they need outside help—for example, using a telephone at the store down the street or at a nearby friend or neighbor's house, or having an agreement in place for someone to leave the house to cool off. Every family member needs to know exactly what will happen if a crisis occurs.

Family-based programs have counselors on call twenty-four hours a day, seven days a week. Each program handles availability differently; sometimes each counselor is always on call, and sometimes the responsibility alternates among staff. The person on call has been briefed about the program's families and is familiar with their issues. A worker who senses an impending crisis with a client should brief the person on call about the situation.

Most of these programs operate on beeper systems, which poses three stumbling blocks: (1) beeper systems need pushbutton telephones to operate and many clients have rotary telephones, (2) some clients do not have telephones at all so cannot access a beeper; and (3) there is no guarantee that the person on call will be able to speak the languages of all clients.

Each program has its own policy about whether counselors should give out their home telephone numbers. Some programs leave the decision up to the counselors; others say it's mandatory to give the number out, and others say it's mandatory *not* to give it out, instead giving clients the program's telephone number to call in a crisis. The family should be informed of the policy.

An Ecological Systems Approach

A family is part of a larger system. To work with only the family and not take the larger social system into consideration is analogous to delivering services to only one family member and ignoring others. Just as the best way to help family members is to involve the entire family, the best way to help a family is to involve all of the systems that interact with it. In this ecological systems approach, the worker's job is to advocate, negotiate, and facilitate comprehensive services.

Although everyone is concerned with the goal of coordination, operationalizing it is surely a challenge. High-risk families typically have so many helpers that coordination can break down at numerous points. Moreover, each worker usually represents a different discipline and is typically a specialist, with certain values and practices. If each person works independently, service provision will likely be inadequate.

Establishing a Coordinated Service Delivery System

The first task for a new family-based program is to contact the various systems with which the program will interface—schools, courts, police, mental health—so they will be aware of it. Developing positive collegial relationships with the agencies with which their families will be likely to interact will lay the groundwork for good working relationships among agencies and good communication. Inviting individuals from these agencies to participate in in-house staff training regularly creates understanding about how the program works, establishes an informal atmosphere, and encourages staff from each organization to develop relationships. It is especially important that those making referrals to the program recognize the criteria for referral and understand what the program can offer.

For their part, workers need to know what other systems are involved with a family so they can initiate contact with *all* significant people involved and coordinate and orchestrate service delivery. Service coordination is important to ensure that all agencies working with a family agree on goals; agree on a treatment plan with the family that will define the role and functions of all those involved; and make sure that the family is not confused by conflicting interventions.[18] When responsibility for service delivery is centralized in one agency, treatment is coordinated and service is comprehensive, integrated, and continuous. The worker maintains ongoing periodic contact with involved agencies to let them know that she is available if problems develop and to update them on the family's progress.

Family-based programs coordinate services in a number of ways. In most programs, workers determine coordination on a case-by-case basis. Some programs like the Lower East Side Family Union (LESFU), implement formal written agreements to clarify the roles of each involved agency and make sure that families receive the services they need. The LESFU, located in one of the poorest sections of New York City, was created in 1972 in response to a fragmented, poorly coordinated, often conflictual service system. The LESFU has three goals: to help families locate and obtain needed services through a case management approach; to coordinate, integrate, and monitor the services provided; and to offer direct services such as homemaking, advocacy, and counseling.

After releases of information have been obtained from the family, the worker and the other involved agencies exchange information in their effort to help the family. The agencies can provide important information about the way a family interacts in settings that the worker would not otherwise have the opportunity to observe; the worker can provide agencies with a perspective that comes from having worked with family members in their home and having developed a trusting relationship. Acting as an intermediary, the worker's goal is to portray the family's strengths to involved agencies. It is important to change the negative opinions that agencies have about multi-need families while simultaneously changing the negative impressions families have about agencies.

Using Formal and Informal Community Resources

The worker acts as an advocate for the family, rebuilding and redefining the family's relationships with community resources. The first step in this process is to help the family overcome any negative feelings they may have toward the community in general or a particular agency within the community—attitudes that are often mutual. By arranging an informal meeting at the family's home with a worker from the agency that the family feels negatively about, the worker is helping both parties gain a better understanding of the other's positions. One author believes "this liaison role may be more important than . . . other more direct efforts with the family."[19] Additionally, the worker is teaching family members how to use relevant community resources to meet their needs.[20]

Rather than simply referring the family to a resource, the counselor accompanies them, acting as both role model and advocate. The worker prepares family members as to what to expect and coaches them on how to navigate an agency's often bureaucratic maze. For example, a worker may accompany parents to a meeting with a school psychologist, teacher, and principal to discuss their child's behavioral problem. He provides support by preparing parents for the questions they may be asked in the meeting (such as "How do you discipline your children at home?"), encouraging them to share information that might be helpful to school personnel, and helping parents to ask questions about their child's behavior in school. Since some parents may become nervous or intimidated, it is helpful to have them write down their questions.

Before they use a resource, the counselor prepares family members. For example, if a child is referred to a play therapy group, the parents need to understand the relevance of play therapy. Often a counselor must do considerable work with the family before they are ready for referral. If referrals are made before a family is motivated to make use of them, services will not help. The counselor also prepares the service to which a family is referred to ensure that the family is well-received. The goal is to make this a positive experience for the family.

From the beginning of their relationship, the worker acknowledges and plans for the time when the family will be on its own, helping and encouraging the family to use various sources of support, both formal (state and private agencies, hospitals, schools, day care) and informal (extended family, friends, neighbors, community organizations, religious organizations, self-help groups). Self-help groups are an excellent source of support for families who are willing to use them. Some of the best known are Parents Anonymous, for abusive parents; Alcoholics Anonymous or Narcotics Anonymous, for substance abusers; and Ala-Anon and Ala-Teen, for relatives of substance abusers. If the community has no such groups, the family-based program staff members can try to start some.

Becoming Advocates

Taking an ecological approach is critical because the environment in which families live shape their view of the world; their lives are inextricably linked to their neighborhoods. Yet few family-based programs become involved in community organizing or social action to address such community-wide problems as drugs, violence, and substandard housing conditions. By virtue of being involved with so many service systems, the worker has the vantage point of seeing where there are gaps in service and strives to accomplish two goals simultaneously: organize the community and motivate families to become involved in changing the environment in which they live.

True empowerment comes when families influence their environment. They make a difference in their community and gain self-esteem and self-confidence. An example is to invite previously homeless families to a meeting at city hall to support the creation of a shelter for homeless families. A family member who testifies to the need for such a program based on her own experience is taking a big step, especially if she has never spoken publicly before. Or, take the example of a previously homeless woman who got a job advocating for homeless families and keynoted a legislative breakfast, talking about the effects of homelessness on her own family. Multi-need families usually do not find themselves in the role of "helper." If they can do something, no matter how small, to help others and to help their community, this benefits both the helper and the recipient.

Problem-Solving and Conflict-Resolution Skills

Most high-risk families need to improve their problem-solving and conflict-resolution skills. The worker embarking on the task of teaching these skills has various approaches to choose from, though all have similar basic steps: (1) recognition of the problem or conflict, (2) definition of the problem or conflict, (3) generation of possible solutions, (4) evaluation of solutions and decision about which is best, (5) decision about how to implement the solution or resolution, and (6) assessment of how well the solution resolved the problem or conflict.[21] Worksheets listing these steps can be a useful tool to the family setting out to resolve a problem. A timetable can be useful as well.

Once again, the worker's role here is as facilitator, not expert. The worker involves the family in the process, from identifying problems to generating solutions, drawing on previous problem-solving successes. The worker thus creates a framework in which the family can creatively solve problems, both within and outside the family, encouraging them to practice using the problem-solving model.

Safety issues are always a consideration when problem solving with family members. (Problem-solving and conflict-resolution skills should *not* be used with families in which there is domestic violence, for reasons explained in Chapter 6.) The first step to ensuring safety is to develop a plan with the family as to how family members will deal with their anger. Laying the ground rules for meetings creates safety. The second step is to structure the physical space in such a way that each family member can easily leave the room if an argument becomes heated. If there is any question of violence, the third step is to bring a co-counselor along. The extra person enhances physical safety and also models cooperation and problem solving by the co-counselors. If one counselor is male and the other female or they come from different ethnic groups, the role modeling assumes an additional dimension of cooperation between sexes or ethnic groups.

Careful structuring of meetings—setting ground rules that include no verbal abuse, no blaming statements, and limiting the amount of time family members can speak to each other—contributes to safety. Teaching the family how to talk in "I" messages decreases blaming. If anger escalates, the worker can defuse the situation by telling family members that they can talk directly only to the worker, making her the switchboard for communication during the meeting. If the tension continues to build, the worker needs to ask everyone to go to separate rooms, giving the worker the opportunity to calm each person down. The worker then meets individually with each family member and all family members agree to meet again as a family to discuss the issue. It may take several meetings before a solution is reached.

Teaching family members to handle their own problems and conflicts will go a long way toward building their self-esteem, self-control, and independence. They will be able to take care of their own issues instead of needing the assistance of social workers, therapists, or probation officers.

Confrontation

Confrontation is a strong intervention strategy that should be used only infrequently because family preservation emphasizes working from strengths, not deficits. Nevertheless, some families have behaviors that the worker must confront.

No confrontation should take place until the counselor has established a strong relationship with the family. Only when family members care about what the worker thinks can confrontation be an effective intervention to motivate people to change their behaviors.

The confrontation itself is carried out with respect. The worker's tone of voice is neutral, and his emotions are under control. He begins by asking family members if they are willing to discuss some concerns that he has. Most members will say yes, but there is usually one person who will become scared or defensive at the mention of concerns. When this happens, the worker has a discussion with the person about why he or she feels defensive or scared, before proceeding with the confrontation. Sometimes the family already knows what these concerns are.

The worker's confrontation is honest, nonjudgmental, and very specific, all the while conveying a message of caring, hope, capability. The concern is framed in a solvable way, so the family feels as if they can do something about it. A worker comes ready to problem-solve with a family and is able to help them seek other services if necessary. Confrontation is most effective when a plan to deal with the issue is agreed upon by the family and is implemented immediately.

A worker may, for example, confront a parent about dysfunctional parenting behaviors (e.g., hitting, yelling, verbal and emotional abuse) she possibly learned from her own parents. She may not even realize that her own parents had been abusive, and thus the goal of the confrontation is to challenge this parent's distorted view of her own childhood, in order to help her understand how her children must feel. Growth and change can occur only when this parent has acknowledged both that her parents' style was abusive and that she has adopted this style with her own children.

Create a Sense of Community Within the Program

Multineed families commonly feel alienated from the larger social system—devalued by people, organizations, and even social service agencies. The worker's role is to help the family become integrated into the mainstream and develop a sense of community which brings with it a sense of belonging and connection.

Changing the family's perception of themselves is the first step. One way to do this is to create a sense of belonging within the program through organized outings—a cookout, a visit to the park, a day at the beach—that are fun and have no treatment focus or celebrations, such as a potluck dinner at Christmastime, with each family member bringing a grab gift to be exchanged at the party. One program we know holds an annual and very popular cookout attended by families currently and previously in the program. Families who have graduated from this program start calling early in the spring to find out the date.

Creating a sense of community with past as well as current families sets a positive example for families in the program. They see that they are not alone, and that life can and will get better, demonstrated so well by families who have successfully terminated and gone on to manage their lives. When a program creates a sense of community, families have a chance to interact with others who have felt similar feelings and have had similar experiences. Together these families begin to change their image of themselves and the community's image of them.

Inviting individuals from other agencies with which the families are involved to program events lets everyone interact in an informal, nonthreatening setting. It also lets agency individuals "catch these families doing something right" when their primary contacts have been largely around crises.

A program newsletter promotes a sense of community. It can include articles by family members, children's drawings, recipes, birth announcements, birthdays, graduations, and announcements of free activities. Another way to develop a sense of community is to have families put together collages of things they're proud of and then frame these, displaying them either at the program or in their homes. The program thus serves as an extended family, offering families respect, encouragement, and hope.

Families are consumers of service. In keeping with a model of mutual respect and collaboration, staff encourage families to evaluate services, pointing out the strengths and weaknesses and making suggestions for improvement. If services are responsive, they become consumer driven. Once family members have graduated from the program, they can be invited to serve on boards or advisory groups or be hired as workers—demonstrating to family members that their opinions are valued and that they can play a role in decision making.

Multidimensional Interventions

High-risk families require multidimensional interventions: recreational activities, budgeting, nutritional education and meal preparation, and rehabilitative services such as individual, group, or family counseling. Studies repeatedly reveal that comprehensive, multidimensional interventions are more effective than a single method.[22] Offering a varied array of developmental and rehabilitative services is critical.

Workers bring a repertoire of skills to their work with families; there is no magical answer or solution, and relying on a single intervention is a mistake. Blending approaches and using multiple strategies have "multiple concurrent effects at different levels—i.e. cognitive, interpersonal, family, and community-wide."[23] Treatment is tailored to address the needs of each family, capitalizing on a spectrum of diverse services.

In addition to multidimensional interventions, creativity is key to effective service delivery, as the Porter family's experience shows. They were referred to the mental health center's family preservation program when ten-year-old Jim became withdrawn and depressed. His mother, Dora, forty nine years old, had seven children and often felt overwhelmed by their many needs. Dora lived with forty-eight-year old Jack, father to her youngest child, who was just two. Only one other child, seven years old, lived at home. The other four children were either married or living on their own yet they continued to expect Dora to meet their needs. They called her every day, expected her to buy them food and clothes, regularly stopped by for meals, and assumed she would watch their children. Dora realized that she needed to stop doing everything for everybody and asked for assistance in setting boundaries. The worker suggested that Dora notify her older children of her decision to resign from her caretaker role in order to focus on her younger children. Dora jumped at the worker's suggestion; she wrote and mailed each of her older children a letter of resignation.

The worker follows the family's lead, offering services tailored to address concerns that they identify. The ability of the worker to facilitate access to a diverse array of services, informal and formal, will benefit the family in two ways: by responding to the many diverse needs of family members and by connecting family members with resources instead of encouraging dependency on the worker.

Specific Treatment Approaches

For high-risk families, an ecological systems approach can be used in combination with a structural approach, communication theory, social learning theory, reality therapy, or solution-focused brief therapy.[24] Programs using diverse treatment modalities may be equally effective. "Developmentally, the field is a long way from determining the best unilateral approach. . . . None of the theories are wrong they are just incomplete."[25] The critical component of treatment is not a particular approach or technique; it is the creation of a trusting relationship between worker and family.

Structural family therapy is well suited for work with high-risk families.[26] It offers staff a useful framework in which to assess and treat families while considering them within the context of their environment. Structural family therapy takes the focus off the identified client and puts the parents in charge. It also identifies family structure and focuses on the family's communication patterns. "In the home-based services world," says one author, "the structural approach to family treatment is the most widely used and, next to social learning, the best tested approach."[27]

Communication theory deals with dysfunctional communication within the family and between the family and their environment. Since dysfunctional communication inhibits effective problem solving, emphasis is placed on teaching communication skills. A number of authors address the importance of improving communication among family members, recommending specific interventions.[28] In *Counseling the Culturally Different*, Sue and Sue point out that both structural and communications approaches appear applicable in work with various minority groups.[29]

Social learning theory and a behavioral approach are the choice of many family preservation programs. Social learning approaches use parent training, role modeling, coaching, contracts, and time-out. Parents find behavior management tools useful in setting clear limits with their children. A behavioral model delineates clear, measurable, and tangible goals; progress is apparent and can be reinforced. Parents are viewed as having skill deficits and can learn to regain authority by controlling rewards and consequences. Once a behavioral plan is developed, parents can learn how to use it. A worker serves as role model, teaching parents how to follow the plan in their home. Role playing, coaching, practice, encouragement, feedback, and reinforcement are taught. Teaching these skills in the family's home is optimal and highly advantageous, enabling parents to practice new skills in the environment in which they will be used instead of translating them from an office setting. Many authors emphasize the importance of social learning approaches and document their effectiveness.[30]

Reality therapy is highly compatible with the core philosophical principles of family preservation. Recognizing that family members are unable to fulfill their basic needs, a counselor helps them meet their needs within the context of a caring relationship. In his book *Reality Therapy*, William Glasser maintains that unless the counselor becomes involved with the client, there is no therapy.[31] Within the context of their relationship, the counselor helps family members face reality. Reality therapy is much like reparenting; the counselor establishes a sincere, trusting relationship with the family, believing in and continually validating family members and helping them to assume responsibility. Focusing on the present instead of the past, reality therapy emphasizes behavioral as opposed to attitudinal change, with the belief that attitudinal change will follow.

Solution-oriented brief therapy has principles that are useful and adaptable to work with high-risk families. It changes the contextual framework in which counselors view families, focusing on identifying and amplifying whatever strengths a client has. For example, if a client has a drug problem and smokes marijuana every night but skipped a night last week, the counselor emphasizes the behavior that was an exception to the problem: the client went one night without smoking. The counselor sincerely and copiously praises the client, pointing out this strength, and with the client tries to determine how he obviated the problem behavior that particular night. The goal is to emphasize this positive act in an effort to determine what the client did differently so that he will repeat the behavior more often and for a longer period of time. The counselor repeatedly acknowledges that whatever this client did was the solution to the problem, if only for a minute, an hour, or a day. The counselor amplifies and builds on this success. "It is easier to enlarge on the existing change, however small, than to create something that does not exist."[32] A small change can affect an entire family system. Thus, the premise that it is more expedient to devise solutions than to stop or change a negative behavior. Solution-focused therapy addresses the effects of problems without dwelling on and belaboring the problems themselves. It is positively oriented, believing that people have the strengths and resources to deal with their problems. It is also future oriented, rendering it unnecessary to know the cause or function of a problem in order to solve it. Finally, it stresses the importance of having clients define their own goals.[33]

Support Groups: Adjuncts to Family Counseling

Support groups are an integral adjunct to family treatment. Parent support groups, adolescent activity groups, mother and child play groups, and family activity groups, among others, not only provide treatment but also create a sense of belonging and community for families, decreasing their social and sometimes geographic isolation.

Groups can be time limited or open-ended. Time-limited groups have two advantages. First, potential participants often feel more comfortable knowing that the group is structured within a particular time frame and that there are beginning and ending dates, as opposed to an ongoing commitment. Second, setting an end date teaches participants how to terminate positively. Group members have a chance to say good-bye to others who have been through a meaningful experience with them. In open-ended groups, terminations occur individually as people leave the group; in time-limited groups, everyone terminates together, heightening the bond or camaraderie among group members.

Parent support groups educate, nurture, and offer socialization and recreation. It is helpful for parents to realize that other parents face similar problems. Participation guarantees parents a break from their children and ensures that parents set time aside for themselves to reflect on their parenting styles and their own lives. Parents look forward to the groups because they are informational, offer a place to discuss concerns, and provide both support and helpful suggestions. Group participation also gives parents the opportunity to help other parents resolve their problems, a role often unfamiliar to them. Typically a real caring develops among members of the group; some develop long-lasting friendships. Thus, parents create a larger support system for themselves. Before initiating a parent support group, workers take into consideration the need for transportation and child care.

Single parents have unique needs. Groups specifically for them can provide support regarding child rearing, discipline, behavior management, handling anger, maintaining adult relationships, and stress management. Being a single parent can be a lonely and tiring experience; there is no one else to take over for the parent who is tired, sick, or simply needs a break from the stress and emotional strain. For working single parents, there is the daily stress of balancing work and home. Talking openly about the frustrations of single parenthood comes more easily for some than others; the group setting lets a parent listen until she feels comfortable enough to talk. Organized recreational activities (a visit to the park, the zoo, a picnic, playing basketball) for a new group helps put parents at ease. These activities give parents the opportunity to interact with each other in informal and enjoyable settings, enabling them to develop relationships.

Adolescent activity groups give teenagers an opportunity to meet and interact. They are also an excellent vehicle to enhance adolescent self-esteem. Activities such as rock climbing, hiking, and camping are effective in developing trust among group members as they learn the importance of relying on someone. More casual opportunities are also appropriate for this age group: playing cards or board games, going to sports events, or visiting local museums. The relationship between the worker and adolescents develops more quickly when the worker participates in activities with youth.

Parent and child play groups are beneficial for parents with young children and are being used by early intervention programs around the country. They teach parents about physical, emotional, and cognitive development and help parents stimulate their child's development. Many groups allocate an hour for the parent and child to participate in an organized activity and then use the second hour to meet with the parent alone while staff play with the children. These groups not only educate parents but also teach them how to have fun with their children, an especially valuable benefit for parents in high-risk families, many of whom do not play with their children because they are overwhelmed just trying to survive. This time affords both parents and children the opportunity to relax and enjoy each other.

Family activity groups are an informal way in which to teach families how to have fun. All families in the program are invited to become involved in casual and informal activity groups that encourage participation in shared activities, such as camping, hiking, playing sports, or cooking meals together. These groups offer a means of reinforcing positive family functioning, teaching families how to play together and how to enjoy themselves. Family activity groups encourage different types of relationships among family members, with youngsters and parents joining together in positive ways. In addition, workers and families have the opportunity to get to know each other while partaking in fun activities instead of focusing on serious problems.

Termination

Termination is rarely given the importance it deserves, yet the entire treatment process is a progression or continuum toward termination. Termination should be carefully planned because it can determine whether a family maintains the gains it has made and can influence a family's willingness to obtain assistance in the future. Positive termination occurs when the family has met its goals, is coping well, has a network of formal and informal support services in place, and a child is no longer at risk of placement.

Termination can seem like a punishment to a family that is doing well and making significant progress. The "reward" for being successful is not only losing services but also losing the relationship with the worker. One way to minimize this perception is to discuss termination from the start of the program, with both worker and family jointly determining termination criteria. This work prepares families for termination, giving them a structured process by which to assess and measure their progress throughout treatment. Formal progress reviews can be scheduled at three-, six-, and nine-month intervals, or more frequently, depending on the length of treatment. During each review, the family and worker talk about the goals that have been accomplished. If the family is having difficulty in a particular area, there is a discussion about what is causing the problem and how the family thinks they can address this dilemma.

Holding regularly scheduled progress reviews encourages a family to succeed at small tasks, receive formal acknowledgment and reinforcement from the worker, and determine what they would like to accomplish next. Goals can be revised or added at the progress reviews. The worker and family devise a timetable for meeting goals, delineating what the worker and each family member must do to attain each goal. Family members can clearly see their progress if it is in writing and discussed openly.

To determine whether a family is ready and willing to terminate, the worker and family must answer the following questions:

- Is the family able to cope with its problems?
- Has the family accomplished the goals it set out to reach when treatment began, or is the family progressing toward the achievement of these goals?
- Are the family's basic needs being met (health, housing, food, a stable source of income)?
- Has the family established a connection with other sources of formal and informal support (friends, extended family, church support groups, self-help groups, private and public agencies)?
- Is the child safe and no longer at risk of out-of-home placement? *or* Has

the child been reunited with the family, and has the family dealt with the issues that caused placement?

This list can be added to by families and workers to best determine readiness for termination.

Once the family and worker agree to terminate, they devise a plan to prepare that includes a termination date and an agreement on the number and frequency of meetings before that date. The termination process entails highlighting the family's accomplishments during treatment and discussing the family's plans for the future. Together the family and the worker consider problems the family may encounter and discuss ways to handle them.

It is critical for the family to have a plan in place to confront potential problems so that they won't lose ground. The plan may include calling the worker or using appropriate services. The conversation about termination also involves a discussion of how the family can continue its progress. The worker doesn't want the family to feel abandoned should setbacks ensue and continually reinforces the family's successes, expressing confidence in their abilities. As appropriate, families are hooked up with informal or formal supports, and the worker helps the family make the transition. The challenge for the worker is to be certain that families are linked with necessary services, with no delay.

Throughout the termination process, the worker encourages the family to discuss and deal with their feelings about termination, which can range from loss to happiness. A family may be proud to complete the program but regret that they have to give up their relationship with the worker. Or they may perceive termination as yet another abandonment and feel angry. They may go into crisis during termination or may experience treatment setbacks. A worker who is able to predict this behavior for the family will be able to allay their fears about termination.

Termination is an important event that needs a celebration—perhaps a dinner at the family's home with the worker bringing a special dish or a party with other program families, with a certificate of completion presented. The symbolic value of a diploma or gift cannot be underestimated. This may be the only diploma a family has ever received or the only time a family has ever had a party celebrating their success. Having staff and families write handwritten notes commending the graduating family on their success is a tangible gift for the family.

The worker refers to the family as graduating (rather than completing or finishing) the program. The term *graduation* implies achievement and moving on to something better, *completion* lacks such positive connotations. The worker helps the family positively terminate by believing in their ability to resolve their own problems. This belief is the worker's final gift to the family.

We must acknowledge that negative terminations do happen. Placement of a child to ensure safety is programmatically perceived as a negative termination (even though it may be in the best interests of the child). Negative terminations also happen when a family decides that family-centered services are not meeting their needs, or program staff or the referring agency contend that the program is not making any progress with the family. If a negative termination occurs, a meeting with the family is scheduled to discuss what the family, worker, and referring agency believe the barriers to treatment may have been. The family is not made to feel that it was their fault that services didn't work; the program model may not have been appropriate to meet their needs. Discussing what the family needs and giving suggestions about where they can find services may prove useful. This enables the family to feel that they can be helped and does not leave them feeling hopeless yet one more time.

6
Special Issues in High-Risk Families

F amily-based services have earned a reputation for successfully working with challenging populations for whom more traditional interventions have proven ineffective. As family problems have grown more severe, family preservation programs around the country continually identify the need for training in such special areas as physical and sexual abuse, domestic violence, substance abuse, HIV/AIDS, homelessness, and reunifying children placed in residential or foster care with their parents. Work in these areas can be demanding, exhausting, and often overwhelming, and counselors who are well prepared will be able to deal with these difficult problems.

Physical and Sexual Abuse

The rate of child abuse increased 50 percent between 1985 and 1992, when 2.9 million cases of maltreatment were reported to child protective agencies.[1] Neglect is the most frequent form of child maltreatment, as the following statistics show: neglect (physical neglect, 8.1 children per 1,000; educational neglect, 4.5 children per 1,000; emotional neglect, 3.2 children per 1,000); physical abuse (4.9 per 1,000); emotional abuse (3.0 children per 1,000); and sexual abuse (2.1 children per 1,000).[2]

Intervening to help children who are physically or sexually abused poses a challenge for all workers. The primary concern is the safety of the child. Decisions about how to proceed are based on extensive and detailed information about the physical or sexual abuse coupled with the family's commitment to change so that the child can remain or return home. Since guidelines for treatment vary for physical and sexual abuse, each is addressed separately.

Treatment of Families with Physically Abused Children

Although each family is unique, with its own set of circumstances, there are certain factors that may enhance the likelihood of physical abuse. Poverty is one of them: "Children from families whose income was less than $15,000 experienced maltreatment almost seven times more frequently than children from higher income families."[3] Poor families have numerous stresses due to their lack of financial resources, lack of education, and lack of job skills. Many of these stressors have been passed from one generation to another, creating a cycle of deprivation that profoundly affects the children of each generation.

Children may be more likely to be at risk of abuse if they are unwanted; are physically ill or are colicky and demanding, making them difficult to care for; or if they resemble someone the parent dislikes (e.g., a hated spouse, lover, or parent). Most physically abusive parents have very low self-esteem, poor impulse control, unrealistic expectations of their children, lack of appropriate parenting skills, little patience with their children, and an inappropriate expectation that their children will meet all their needs for love and affection. These parents are often isolated or have negative relationships with their extended family, so they have no one to turn to for support. Many abusive parents were themselves victims of physical abuse as children. Since parents learn their parenting styles from their families of origin, these parents are at risk of abusing their own children. (However, not all parents who suffered physical abuse as children become abusive parents.)

Problems in the parental and marital relationship can result in physical abuse. A parent may be jealous of the attention his or her partner pays to a particular child, or a parent may be instigated to abuse a child because his or her partner complains that the child is spoiled, or is not disciplined enough, or is out of control. Parents use the child as a scapegoat for the hostilities they feel toward each other but are afraid to express because they fear ending their relationship. When one partner leaves the relationship in the case of separation or divorce, the remaining parent may respond to the children with hostility and anger.

The problem workers face is how to deal with a family in which such abuse occurs. The worker's immediate priority is to determine if the child is safe. One of the considerations is the severity and frequency of the abuse. A parent who is hitting a child regularly can be taught alternative methods of discipline. A child who is being beaten and bruised is another matter. The worker must report the recurrence of abuse to the child protection agency, which may result in out-of-home placement. Decisions concerning child safety are difficult and should not be made without consulting one's supervisor or colleagues, or both.

If the worker determines that the child can remain at home, the next step is to stop the abuse by creating a plan with numerous supports to ensure safety—for example, daily home visits by the worker, having the family identify and designate someone in or outside the family that the abused child can tell if the abuse reoccurs, or creating a written contract with the family. A written contract is a particularly good tool; it must be very specific in terms of acceptable behavior, all family members must sign it, and it must be displayed prominently (e.g., on the refrigerator).

The worker plays a dual role, which is inherently conflictual—that she is there to help yet mandated to report abuse that reoccurs. The family is motivated to change by the possibility of having their child removed; thus, often abuse will abate at least temporarily, giving the worker the opportunity to intervene. In this situation, the worker needs to display a nonjudgmental attitude and listen with genuine concern to what the parents express as their needs. This noncritical, accepting attitude and willingness to listen is a cornerstone of family preservation. Reparenting also plays a role, with the worker responding to the parents' need for nurturing and support. Parents learn that they can count on the worker, and a trusting relationship typically ensues.

It is often useful to encourage the family to give the child permission to talk about the abuse with someone outside the family, thereby dismantling the family secret of abuse. The worker first meets with the parents to suggest this course of action. If the parents agree, they speak to their child, with or without the worker present. This approach serves a dual purpose: it encourages the family to discuss the physical abuse and removes the secrecy surrounding it. For example, during his work with a family-based counselor, a father was worried that he would not be able to stop his physically abusive behavior although he very much wanted to. The worker related a story about an abusive mother who told her child to call the worker if the mother was physically abusive. This story encouraged the father to try the same tack in his family. This was the first step the father took to change his behavior. He also attended a parenting group, where he learned other methods of discipline and anger management skills and was able to share his need to develop more patience with his children.

The counselor teaches physically abusive parents appropriate ways to discipline their children—time out, logical consequences, family rules, and consequences for breaking the rules, for example. Parents can participate in parent education classes or a parent support group to learn alternative methods of discipline, understand the developmental stages of childhood, and realize that other parents have similar problems.

Many physically abusive parents have a misconception of the purpose of discipline; they view it as a way to punish children who fail to obey instructions. The job of workers is to convince parents that discipline is a means by which to *educate* children as to what they can and cannot do. Discipline teaches children what is safe and what is unsafe (e.g., it is not safe to cross the street without first looking in both directions); it imposes limits on children, delineating clear and consistent boundaries, in the hope that they will internalize these boundaries.

The worker helps parents acknowledge that physical abuse not only harms the child but fails to change behavior. In addition to causing serious injuries, physical abuse can also have negative long-range side effects on the child: depression, acting out, violent behavior with peers, and posttraumatic stress syndrome. If physically abusive parents are asked if they think punishment works, they often claim that it doesn't but say that they have to hit their children even more now than ever before. These parents believe that if they increase the physical abuse, they'll get better results. This illogical conclusion necessitates that the worker convince parents that they will get better results by using different discipline methods, not more of the same physical abuse.

Workers must acknowledge that child-rearing practices differ from culture to culture, and certain cultures sanction physical punishment. Although it may be impossible to alter a parent's accepted cultural norm that it is all right to punish one's children physically, workers can influence parents to change their behavior to avoid having their children removed from the family. It is optimal to change a parent's belief system as well as his or her behavior, yet this is not always possible or it may be possible only over time. This is especially difficult in cultures in which violence is condoned.

The example of a Vietnamese-Hmong family who recently settled in a Midwest community characterized by its intolerance of outsiders is illustrative.[4] The mother came out of the grocery store and instructed her six-year-old son to stand beside the shopping cart and watch the groceries while she got the car. Instead, the boy darted across the parking lot, nearly getting hit by a car. His mother beat him until a police officer arrested her in the street for beating her son. The mother was very confused, for in her culture, beating one's child was an acceptable cultural norm, but highly anxious, thinking that she would be deported. She spoke very little English and no translator was available to explain the situation.

The family was referred to a mental health center, and a translator was present who calmed the mother's fears about being deported and told her that if she wanted to "keep the authorities off her back," she had to stop beating her child. The counselor recognized that he needed to be sensitive to the woman's culture while also upholding the law, so instead of initially attempting to change the woman's cultural belief about punishment, he focused on altering her behavior, teaching her alternative methods of discipline and convincing her not to use sticks and switches and not to hit her child in anger. The worker's immediate goal was to lessen the severity of the physical abuse, with the long-range goal of having it taper off completely.

Workers may be adamantly against hitting a child, yet they must conscientiously guard against judging people according to their value system. Child-rearing practices vary dramatically from culture to culture; what is accepted in one culture may be forbidden in another.

Once parents begin to employ alternative methods of discipline and a positive worker-family relationship is established, emphasis is placed on discussing the stresses contributing to physical abuse. "It is not easy to move beyond the symptom of child abuse into the dynamics which have led to it.

When this process becomes possible, what emerges is that often these families have experienced lives similar to any seriously dysfunctional family."[5] Worker and family discuss internal as well as external stressors, such as the impact of homelessness, substance abuse, or unemployment. Emphasis is placed on talking about how parents were disciplined as children. Since physically abusive parents often have unrealistic expectations of their children, the worker helps educate parents about a child's abilities and needs at various stages of development.

Treatment of Families with Sexually Abused Children

Within the family preservation field, there is a dearth of literature on working with families with sexually abused children, so we must rely on family therapy literature for insight into the problem and help for staff who must deal with these families. Staff need extensive training, experience, expertise, and ongoing individual and peer supervision. This work can be emotionally draining, and workers require backup support to test their judgment since the power of denial and severity of dysfunction may be overpowering.

Family-based programs *cannot* deal with all sexual abuse cases; to make such a sweeping generalization would do the family preservation movement a disservice. Not all families that have experienced sexual abuse should stay together or be reunited.

Although the empirical research has been scant, three studies have described the characteristics of incest offenders. One of them, conducted by Dr. David Finklehor and Dr. Linda Meyer Williams, sociologists at the Family Research Laboratory of the University of New Hampshire, and focusing on incestuous fathers, identified five types of incestuous fathers:

1. The Sexually Preoccupied (26 percent of the fathers) had a deliberate and often obsessive sexual interest in their daughters under the age of ten. This group includes a subcategory of fathers who regarded their daughters as sexual objects almost from birth.

2. The Adolescent Regressives (33 percent of the fathers—the largest group) became interested in their daughters just before or when they entered puberty.

3. The Instrumental Self-Gratifiers (20 percent of the fathers) fantasized about someone else while they abused their daughters.

4. The Emotionally Dependent (10 percent of the fathers) were emotionally needy, lonely, and dejected men. The abuse usually began when the children were six or seven years old.

5. The Angry Retaliators (10 percent of the fathers) abused when enraged and sometimes used physical violence too. These fathers were angry at either their daughters or their wives and some abused their daughters because they resembled their mothers.[6]

These researchers had other significant findings:

- Alcohol and drugs were used to lower the fathers' inhibitions to abuse, but only 9 percent claimed that drugs or alcohol were responsible for the abuse.
- Forty-three percent of the men believed that marital problems contributed to the abuse.
- Seventy percent of the offenders had been sexually abused as children.
- Half the men had been physically abused by their fathers and 44 percent by their mothers.

The second study, conducted by Dr. Nicholas Groth, founder of the Sex Offender Program at the Connecticut Correctional Institution, categorized nonviolent offenders as regressed and fixated. Regressed offenders are adult males who are attracted to adult females but may turn to children for sex as a substitute when under stress, such as losing a job or a spouse. Fixated offenders prefer to have sex with children throughout their lives. Fixated offenders are sometimes discovered in families as incest offenders; however, their victims also include children outside the family. It is not unusual for a fixated offender to marry a woman with children in part to have contact with the children.[7]

Ruth Mathews, of Midway Family Services, a program of Family Services of Greater St. Paul, identified four categories of female offenders:

1. Teacher-Lovers: Older women who have sex with adolescents.
2. Experimenter-Exploiters: Typically young adolescent girls from strict families that never discuss sex.
3. Predisposed Abusers: Women who are predisposed to offend because they were sexually abused from a very young age by at least one family member.
4. Male-Coerced Women: Women who are forced by men to abuse children.

Female offenders, she found, take more responsibility for their actions than do their male counterparts, suggesting that female offenders have a better prognosis for treatment.[8]

Most of the literature refers to nonoffending parents as female and perpetrators as male, and so we must therefore limit this discussion to that population. Nonoffending female parents are traditionally dependent and frightened of their partners, have low self-esteem, are terrified of being left without financial support, and may have been sexually abused as children by their fathers. These women were frequently parentified children in their families of origin. They are often emotionally unavailable to their husbands and children. That "a woman who fails to protect her offspring sometimes evokes greater outrage than the offender himself" reflects the attitude of many workers, as well as the general public, toward the nonoffending female parent, who is often blamed and held responsible for her partner's sexual abuse.[9]

Programs must establish protocols for working with families in which there is sexual abuse. Many will not accept a case if the perpetrator is living in the home and it is always inadvisable to do family work if the perpetrator is living in the home and refuses to acknowledge the abuse. Often the nonoffending parent will also deny the abuse. In this situation the worker's only recourse is to tell the family that the child will be placed unless the perpetrator moves out. Removing the child can motivate a family in denial.

First, the safety of the child is addressed. Then, most therapists agree, work must begin with the entire family. If feasible, initial family work should be done while the perpetrator is living apart, with both perpetrator and victim receiving individual therapy. Perpetrators may also participate in offender groups. The counselor then conveys the dramatic message to the family that the family dynamics themselves must change radically. There is typically more going on in the family than the sexual abuse, for these families "tend to be dysfunctional across a wide range of dimensions."[10] Treatment must focus more widely, on issues other than the sexual abuse. For example, although the responsibility for the abuse clearly lies with the perpetrator, a number of variables may set the stage for sexual abuse, such as the marital relationship or issues involving nonabused siblings, and unless the family confronts these issues and develops a new relational model, the risk remains.[11]

Dr. Denise Gelinas, a therapist in private practice specializing in the treatment of incest, has written about the importance of addressing relational issues surrounding incestuous child sexual abuse because "particular relational imbalances characteristically precede incest and are then perpetuated, and new abuses are introduced, by the sexual abuse itself."[12] She conceptualizes the therapeutic work as resting on three basic premises:

1. The adult is always responsible for the sexual contact.
2. The victim is assiduously loyal to his or her parents, and this loyalty must be supported throughout treatment.
3. The adult is held accountable for the sexual abuse, but the therapist must never scapegoat or permit the family to scapegoat.

In sexual abuse cases, Dr. Gelinas recommends using the family therapy technique of multilaterality, in which the therapist considers the needs of each family member but is careful not to align with a particular family member. If, for example, the counselor aligns with the victim against the perpetrator, the victim's loyalty to the perpetrator will come to the forefront and the victim will defend the perpetrator against the counselor. In this situation, the worker's effectiveness as a change agent will plummet.

The sole use of a family treatment approach is inadequate when dealing with fixated offenders, says Gelinas, who recommends supplementing family therapy with individual treatment provided by a counselor experienced in offender work or at least participation in an offenders' group. The counselor must closely monitor the offender's behavior over a long period of time, helping him learn to control his impulses.[13]

The worker initially addresses the denial of family members, which has four stages:

Stage 1—Denial of the Facts. Family members deny that any abuse happened.

Stage 2—Denial of Awareness. Family members deny knowing anything about the abuse. Siblings may say they were never home when the abuse occurred. The perpetrator may claim to have been drunk or high and is unable to remember what happened.

Stage 3—Denial of Responsibility. The child often blames herself or himself during this stage, or the nonoffending parent blames the child, or the perpetrator may claim that the child was seductive.

Stage 4—Denial of Impact. Family members admit the abuse happened and that they knew about it and believe the perpetrator is responsible but minimize the severity or the effects of the abuse on the victim.[14]

Each stage of denial must be addressed and resolved if the family is to heal.

A pressing question for workers is whether the perpetrator who is living apart should be allowed to visit the child. Most family therapy literature supports time-limited supervised visits if the perpetrator is not in denial; permitting visits with a perpetrator in denial leaves a child at risk for confusion and manipulation. A perpetrator who is barred from visiting the child is often motivated to break through denial in order to see the child.

If the situation allows, visits to an offender living apart are important. Otherwise, the child protective system typically blames the perpetrator, and the family defends him. Family loyalty tends to be strong, so keeping the perpetrator involved with the family in a positive way by visits enables the victim to begin to establish a different relationship with the parent in an environment that is closely monitored to ensure that there is no discussion of sexual abuse or retraumatization of the child.

If the perpetrator is still in the home or if the family is being reunified, the counselor ensures that the family assigns someone the job of protecting the child from further abuse—perhaps a grandmother or godmother. Then the worker and family develop a detailed plan in which the perpetrator devises steps to take should the urge to abuse reoccur and a clear contract specifying what will happen if the offender abuses again.

An important step in the victim's healing is the acknowledgment of the abuse by the perpetrator and the entire family. Again we turn to the field of family therapy for a theoretical framework. In her book *Love, Sex, and Violence*, Cloé Madanes has developed a sixteen-step approach for dealing with juvenile sex offenders that can be adapted to other age groups. A major focus of this approach is her dramatization of having the perpetrator get down on his knees to apologize to the victim and promise the abuse will never happen again. This apology occurs in a family meeting, with all family members present. Other family members also apologize to the victim for not providing protection or not believing the child. The apology by other family members does not remove the responsibility from the offender; instead, it serves to acknowledge that family members failed to keep the child safe.[15]

For sibling incest, more prevalent than parent-child incest, many of the issues already noted are applicable.[16] Some family preservation programs refuse to work with juvenile offenders unless they are adjudicated, yet most juveniles are not because parents often refuse to file charges against their own children. Nevertheless, many of these families are motivated to change, and these youngsters must not be ignored. "Child offenders who receive treatment . . . do much better than adults. They need less long-term help and are less likely to reoffend."[17]

Workers must be straightforward and sincere with families dealing with sexual abuse. Too often workers continue to specify family reunification as the treatment goal when all parties know that the family will never be reunited. If the perpetrator is in denial and the prognosis is poor, the worker must be candid with the family, informing them that reunification would endanger the child and is out of the question. If reunification continually appears on a treatment plan and never materializes, a family will become alienated.[18]

Domestic Violence

That more than half of all women will experience some form of spousal violence during marriage and that women in the United States are more likely to be assaulted in their homes than anywhere else is no surprise to helping professionals, who regularly encounter families in which domestic violence occurs.[19] It is not uncommon for battered women to be victimized a second time, after the assault, but now by service providers. Battered women who seek help may find that therapists "rarely identify the problem, minimize its significance, inappropriately medicate and label abused women, provide them with perfunctory or punitive care, [and] refer them for secondary psychosocial problems but not for protection from violence."[20] The worker must be cognizant of her feelings about domestic violence and aware of how these feelings will affect the treatment process. A family-based approach to addressing domestic violence must consider a number of factors relating to all parties to the violence and to the most effective treatment.

The Batterer

Domestic violence is a pattern of coercive control involving intimidation and domination that an abuser utilizes over his victim. (Not only men are batterers but since the vast majority are male, we refer to the batterer as male and the victim as female.) There is a paucity of training available for those who work with men who batter and few treatment programs for batterers within mainstream agencies (e.g., community mental health centers). In addition, there are numerous myths about who batterers are and why they batter, with racial, class, gender, and personality stereotypes abounding. Let's dispel with a few myths:

- Batterers are *not* readily identifiable.
- The frequency of battering in gay and lesbian relationships is similar to that of heterosexual relationships.
- The typical batterer is not mentally ill.
- A substance abuse problem does not make someone become a batterer, and getting clean does not make battering stop.
- A batterer can be of any class; higher education does not make someone less likely to batter.
- The typical batterer is often perceived by people as calm and easygoing and is usually not violent outside of intimate relationships.

Battering is a learned behavior—learned from one's family of origin, from peers, or from the media. Many batterers were abused as children, as were their victims.[21] Research has shown that men who abuse their children often abuse their partners.

The batterer's key issue revolves around ownership and possession; he believes that he "owns" his partner and his children and tends to treat them like objects or possessions, dehumanizing them in order to justify his battering. He believes that he has the right to control his "possessions," and violence is only the most visible part of the abuse, used when all other control strategies have failed. The batterer believes it is his right to have his needs met at any cost. He is highly self-centered and feels entitled to be taken care of physically, emotionally, and sexually. The batterer's goal is to get what he wants, no matter what. Most batterers will deny or minimize their battering and are adept and manipulative, often representing themselves as victims.

For example, a batterer may say, "She kept nagging me, repeatedly bringing up the fact that I never got her a birthday present, so after listening to this over and over again, I hit her a couple of times. If she hadn't nagged and nagged, I never would have hit her."

Working with the Whole Family

The literature suggests that traditional family and couples therapy is inappropriate when addressing domestic violence. A woman who discloses during a couples or family counseling session that she has been battered may suffer even more abuse. Providing couples and family treatment gives the batterer the message that the problem is in his relationship when, in fact, his need to control his partner is the key problem. Batterers are not people who have poor control of their impulses; rather, they have given themselves permission to be abusive within specific parameters. Treatment of the batterer focuses on having him relinquish control over his family, not gaining control of his behavior.

A worker doing an initial interview with the entire family to obtain information about family interactions may suspect domestic violence but should never ask directly about it, for two reasons: a direct question can put the woman and children at risk, and typically the family denies spouse abuse anyway. Open-ended questions, however, can be asked that will give the worker some indication about whether there is abuse in the home—for example, "How do various members of the family handle anger?" A telling answer might be, "My boyfriend screams and hollers, and throws things," accompanied by nervous laughter by the other members. Or such a question might be met with silence. A worker who senses domestic violence must *never* pursue the subject in the family meeting to avoid putting the woman and children at risk. The best response is a follow-up meeting with the woman individually.

Treatment in this situation remains family focused because the worker employs a family systems approach, but the counselor does not work with the entire family. The batterer is not directly informed that he is excluded from meetings; the worker visits the woman alone and schedules meetings when the batterer is unable to attend. If the batterer is present, the worker *never* discusses domestic violence to avoid alienating the batterer. The worker cannot jeopardize the woman or children's safety.

Working with the Victim

A worker suspicious of domestic violence must proceed slowly. Confronting a woman with these suspicions early in treatment may be counterproductive, inhibiting the development of a trusting relationship. It is more likely that the abused woman will disclose the existence of abuse after the establishment of a trusting relationship. When this occurs, the worker can ask probing, open-ended questions: "What did you mean when you said your boyfriend screams and hollers, and throws things?" "What does he throw?" "What does he say when he hollers?" And, if the worker elicits information about violent or intimidating behavior, ask for details: "Did he hit you with an open or closed fist?" "How many times?" "Were there any injuries?" "Did you have to go to the emergency room?" Or the approach may be more subtle: "What happens when he doesn't get his way?" The goal for the worker is to create an atmosphere of openness and be genuinely willing to listen.

Spouse abuse is often a family secret. A victim may be just as concerned as the abuser about others' learning the family's secret of domestic violence. The abused woman is often isolated and may believe that no one cares about her or her story. Thus, once the abuse is revealed, the worker is not critical or judgmental of the abuser but rather is calm and empathetic.

Once the woman has confided that there is abuse, the worker communicates a willingness to help, encouraging the woman to talk about her situation. The worker labels the abuse as abuse, instead of choosing not to address it, a response that would express an indirect form of approval. The worker educates the woman about the dynamics of domestic violence, letting her know that it is not her fault and that the batterer is responsible for his own behavior. The worker validates the woman for disclosing the abuse and lets the woman know she is not alone by sharing stories of women who have left their abusers and changed their lives.

Safety

Whether the woman and children are safe is a difficult decision to make, and one that is very often decided by child welfare agencies and courts instead of families. The typical situation—a child welfare agency removes the children if the abused spouse does not leave the abuser—is counterproductive because it holds the abused woman responsible for the abuser's actions, further blaming and punishing the victim and traumatizing the children, an intervention that parallels and replicates the family's dynamics.

Any effort to assess the woman and children's safety must consider the type, severity, and frequency of the abuse to determine if the violence is escalating. This can be done by asking about the first, the last, and the worst incident of abuse. The worker also learns if the abuser has access to weapons. Then the worker and abused woman explore options that will not separate her from her children, such as shelters, legal assistance, counseling, or attending a support group for abused women. Support groups are especially useful; the woman finds that other women have had the same experience, and they can encourage her to consider options to staying in the relationship. Through participation in a support group, an abused woman may find enough strength to make the decision to leave her abuser. If the worker believes that the children are in a life-threatening situation and that their mother is unable to keep them safe, the only option is to notify the child protective agency.

Most abused women initially are unwilling to make any changes. The worker's role is to express genuine concern for the woman's safety and give her information and support for exploring alternatives and resources. The worker can ask what she can do to ensure the woman's safety and her children's too. Children can be considered victims of domestic violence even if they are not the direct target; they often have such problems as difficulty in school, delinquency, enuresis, and nightmares.

Treatment Goals and Interventions

The worker and the abused woman jointly determine the goal of treatment, with the woman explaining what she wants and the worker following her lead, consistent with the family preservation principle that the worker does not dictate treatment goals. Taking the decision out of the woman's hands would reinforce her feelings of powerlessness and inability to protect herself and her children. Women who have left abusive relationships often identify the caring and support of a worker who stuck with them until they felt ready to leave their abusive partners as the most important assistance they were offered. Believing in these women and caring about them gives them hope.

A worker may encounter criticism from colleagues and other service providers for supporting a woman who stays with her abusive partner; many believe that the worker should give the woman ultimatums to leave in order to protect herself and her children. Certainly the worker's values and patience will be challenged if the woman remains in an abusive relationship, yet the worker acknowledges that persuading the woman to leave is counterproductive and potentially dangerous: Abused women are in the greatest danger when they are trying to leave a relationship. The worker cannot accurately predict how dangerous a batterer might be and since the abused woman suffers the consequences of whatever course of action she chooses, it is not up to the worker to jeopardize the woman's safety by insisting that she leave.

Encouraging the abused woman to go through the steps of problem solving (see Chapter 5) brings structure to an overwhelming and seemingly hopeless situation and identifies possibilities. Knowing the resources in the community and helping women use them is critical. Another intervention option is to do safety planning with women who decide to stay in their relationships. The abused woman and the worker develop a plan to keep herself and her children safe, perhaps staying with an identified friend if she needs to leave immediately, so if a crisis arises, the woman knows exactly what to do. The majority of abused women decide to stay with the batterer; developing a safety plan responds to their reality and represents a shift in thinking, in that the focus in the past was on convincing women to leave their relationships.

The treatment options for batterers are limited. Individual, couples, and family work are inappropriate treatment modalities. In individual treatment, the batterer can manipulate the therapist into believing that he has a relationship problem. Couples and family work implies to the abuser that his violence stems from problems in his relationship. And, as noted, many women are battered after these sessions. There are programs specifically for batterers, with treatment conducted through groups comprised of other batterers, but success rates are disheartening. It appears that short-term gains are significant, but the ability of the batterer to sustain long-term change is limited, with battering often beginning again a year or two later. Like sex offenders, batterers have a high rearrest rate, and their capacity for change is limited. Abused women need to be told that short-term change is common but that long-term change is atypical. Short-term change can create false hope in women who want to believe that the change is permanent.

If a batterer does decide to participate in a program, the family worker regularly communicates with staff at the batterer's program to assess his progress and exchange information. The worker also checks with the batterer's partner, for only she can offer an accurate assessment of whether the batterer's behavior has changed.

Dealing with domestic violence can be especially difficult, stressful, and traumatic for workers. It is mandatory that they receive ongoing training and supervision to prevent overidentification and vicarious traumatization (experiencing trauma as a result of working with these families). Supervision is particularly important when a worker learns of domestic violence and realizes she must be careful not to discuss the issue with the woman's partner. The worker may feel uncomfortable and anxious about being in this predicament; supervision will provide a place to deal with the dilemma.

Substance Abuse and HIV/AIDS

Most family-based programs report a high incidence of alcohol and drug abuse among their clients, and the consequences affect the entire family: "Families experiencing alcohol problems have a 40 percent divorce rate. There are 5.7 million cases a year of family violence linked to alcohol abuse."[22] Studies indicate that substance-abusing parents are more likely to abuse their children, with alcoholic fathers eight times more likely and alcoholic mothers three times more likely to abuse or neglect their children than nonalcoholic parents.[23] Substance abuse clouds judgment and self-control, increasing the risk for child abuse and neglect, incest, and other family violence. There are other serious problems as well. When parents are asked how they think their substance abuse affects their parenting, they say that they are not often emotionally present for their children; for example, when they are high, they turn on the television so that they don't have to interact with their children. Additionally, if they fall asleep and leave the children unsupervised, the children's safety is compromised. Sometimes they leave their children with people who are irresponsible and do not adequately care for them. A final problem is that increasing numbers of infants and young children are becoming involved in the child welfare system as a result of parental substance abuse. Every year approximately 375,000 infants are born drug abused, and since 1985 the incidence of substance abuse during pregnancy has increased threefold.[24]

Counselors who work with substance-abusing families seek to facilitate a family's recognition of the effect of substance abuse on their lives and encourage them to discuss it. At the same time, the counselor must ensure child safety. Some counselors believe that no work can be accomplished with a substance abuser until that person is clean and that working with the substance abuser's family in the interim is unproductive. We disagree. There is much that can be done with the substance-abusing family member and with other family members.

A family-based approach is effective with these families. Because services are provided in the home, substance abuse can quickly be detected and child safety realistically assessed and monitored. Family-based services support family members, encouraging them to attend such groups as Al-Anon, while concomitantly suggesting to the substance abuser that if he or she thinks there is a problem, treatment is available. The support of a home-based worker can encourage a family member's decision to disclose substance abuse or seek treatment.

Workers begin by assessing strengths; the family is discouraged and hopeless, and there is not much they can initially do about the substance abuser. It makes more sense to look at how the family has coped under tense and stressful conditions. The worker also helps family members recognize the function their roles serve in the family—chief enabler, hero, scapegoat, lost child, mascot.[25] (The chief enabler, usually the spouse of the substance abuser, is responsible for maintaining the status quo. The hero, often the oldest child, takes responsibility for portraying the family as normal to the outside world. The scapegoat, typically a middle child, continually gets into trouble, taking the focus off the substance abuser in an effort to keep the family together. The lost child, usually a middle or youngest child, appears invisible to the family. The mascot, usually the youngest child, acts as comedian to take the stress off the family.) The family may not at first understand how the roles they play hold the family together. This is why involvement with a self-help group is useful; it helps family members recognize the patterns of addiction and realize that they are not alone. Their lives revolve around adjusting their behavior to accommodate the substance abuser, becoming codependent in an effort to keep the family together no matter what. Acknowledging family roles lays the groundwork for change. When families begin to understand their roles, they often decide they want to change them, moving forward in treatment.

Once the family acknowledges that a substance abuse problem exists, the worker educates them about the addiction and how it affects the whole family. The worker can suggest that the family attend self-help groups. If family members are anxious about going alone, uneasy about meeting new people, or lack transportation, the worker can go with them. This partnership facilitates the development of a trusting relationship and enables the worker to learn more about the effects of addiction on the family.

It may be useful to hold a family meeting in which family members tell the substance abuser the effect his or her behavior has had on them. Their stories can be an eye opener. Substance abusers may be oblivious to the effect of this behavior on family members; sometimes they even think no one else knows about it. Once the secret is out in the open, the family is capable of making changes. Family members may suggest that the abuser seek treatment but not try to convince or force him or her to do so.

The worker's role is to support family members in confronting and acknowledging their problems and help them find additional services, *not* to get the substance abuser into treatment. It's unrealistic to think that workers can successfully motivate every substance abuser to pursue treatment. If work with the family is limited to having the family acknowledge the problem, then at least the process has begun. Sometimes only a single family member is needed to deal with the issue to make a difference. If one member changes his or her response to the family problem, other family members have to adapt, creating change in the family. Nevertheless, much work may need to be done before the abuser obtains any treatment. For example, during a parent support group for single mothers in a state-funded program for families of adolescents, one of the mothers admitted to being a "prescription junkie." The discussion that followed centered on how the mother's addiction affected her family, especially her daughter, who was a runaway and involved in illegal activities. Other mothers offered their support to her and expressed concern for her well-being. In answer to the worker's question about how the group wanted to deal with this admission, they decided they wanted to be available to this mother, but asked her to try not to be under the influence of drugs when she attended the group. During the next nine months, this mother regularly attended group meetings and never arrived under the influence. One night she announced that she had decided to enter treatment to begin to deal with her addiction and asked for support from group members and assistance in locating an appropriate treatment program. The worker helped with a referral, and the woman entered a program within the week.

Counselors who work with addicted clients must avoid the danger of becoming codependent. It's very easy to begin to enable or take care of the substance abuser or other family members. A worker who tries to make everyone happy and fix everything is not helping the family but instead enabling the substance abuser to continue to abuse and making it less likely that he or she will seek treatment.

One of the grimmest consequences of substance abuse is AIDS. The victims are intravenous drug users, their sexual partners, and children who are infected with the human immunodeficiency virus in utero.[26] Not all infants born to mothers with AIDS are infected, but they are at high risk. Sometimes mothers learn that they are HIV infected when their child is diagnosed with AIDS. The diagnosis comes as a shock to most families, and they often react with guilt and shame.

The family-based model provides in-home services and is thus a possible treatment modality for families in which there is HIV/AIDS. Establishing a trusting partnership with these families is key. Because of the stigma associated with HIV/AIDS, families often keep the illness secret, often not even telling extended family or friends. They become socially isolated and without support. The nonjudgmental posture integral to family-centered work is instrumental in forming a relationship with a family in which there is HIV/AIDS. Working with these families means addressing a combination of practical as well as emotional issues. It necessitates more than just doing treatment, requiring attention to many practical and concrete details.

If one or both parents are HIV infected, they need to consider when and how to tell their children about their disease and determine what supports or services the children may need. Parents are concerned about what will happen to their children after their death, so early in treatment and while the infected person is still well, the worker assists the parent in drawing up a will and in deciding who will become the children's guardian. This decision is often difficult, for a parent who may be in denial about the illness; the worker may need to help the parent work through denial before further issues can be addressed.

In some families, the worker will not only have to deal with HIV/AIDS parents, but also an infected child. "Some level of denial is necessary for parents and professionals caring for HIV-infected children. This reaction reduces the negative effect of the illness and enables parents to mobilize their strengths for the difficult course of the illness."[27] Both parents and professionals need to have enough hope to enable them to cope. Slipping into hopelessness would only sap their strength, and they need all the strength they can mobilize. Denial can, however, create a problem when it paralyzes or inhibits parents from accessing medical services for their children. As better medical treatment becomes available, children with HIV who used to live to be three years old are now living until they are seven or eight. The fact that these children are living longer creates a whole new set of considerations that demand attention.[28] When infected children died very young, they interacted solely with their family and the medical system. Now, families are forced to deal with the negative reactions of the educational system and the community to the fact that their child is HIV infected. It is not uncommon for these children to keep their illness a secret, yet they require a good deal of support and encouragement. If the trend of prolonging the lives of HIV-infected children continues, these children will reach puberty. At this point, education about relationships and "safe sex" will need to be made available to the family. HIV-infected adolescents will want to have relationships with their peers which means that their sexual behavior must be discussed as well as their impending death from AIDS.

Elisabeth Kübler-Ross's five stages of dying—denial, rage and anger, bargaining, depression, and acceptance—offers a useful framework for both workers and families to understand the process that families experience.[29]

Helping the family learn to live with a disease, as opposed to focusing on dying, is a critical goal of treatment. Together with the family, the worker addresses concrete needs: food, housing, transportation to and from medical appointments, and medical services. Helping a family participate in support groups in which they can share their fears and gain strength benefits the entire family by reducing social isolation and creating a support system. Another treatment goal is to coordinate service delivery for the family, ensuring that visiting nurses, hospitals, social services, day care, and hospices communicate in regularly scheduled case conferences. This helps address the chaos a family typically experiences by having so many people involved in their lives.

Workers must be able to deal with an array of emotions that families experience during the illness and after the infected family member dies. This is emotionally demanding and draining work, and counselors engaged in it need support, preferably with a group for professionals working with people with HIV/AIDS.

Homeless High-Risk Families

Homeless high-risk families are becoming one of this country's largest growing populations in need of services. The picture of homelessness changed considerably during the 1980s. Previously made up of primarily homeless individuals, the homeless population in the United States now comprises many families—more than one-third of all homeless people. Additionally, approximately 5 million families are potentially homeless, living with friends and relatives.[30]

The primary reason for the significant increase in homelessness and doubled-up families is a lack of affordable housing, which can be attributed to four major causes: lowered federal allocations for low-income housing, rising housing costs, an increase in the number of families living below the poverty line, and increased unemployment. Two other factors contribute to homelessness as well: discrimination by landlords, sellers, and realtors against families with children, despite a law passed by Congress in 1988 banning such discrimination, and domestic violence. "Studies in communities around the country consistently find that between 25 to 50 percent of homeless families left their homes because of domestic violence."[31]

When family homelessness first began, states didn't know how to respond. In the past, many cities put homeless families in barracks-style shelters that afforded little or no privacy. In the 1980s, a number of states created "welfare motels" to shelter families, an enormously costly response. The Martinique, in New York City, charged $63 a night for a family of four, which amounts to $1,900 a month. To rent the family an apartment would have cost only $500 a month.[32] Because of the high cost of welfare motels combined with the unavailability of affordable housing, states began to develop emergency family shelters that typically provided each family with one bedroom, shared showers, cooking facilities, and a communal evening meal. New York City exemplifies the beginning of an elaborate family sheltering system in the United States.

As more and more families entered shelters, it became evident that large numbers of these families had more needs than just permanent housing. "The homeless families of the 1980s may well be the 'multiproblem' families of previous decades, but they are now far more visible."[33] The Gomez family— mother, father, and two children—exemplify the multiproblem family. Mr. Gomez is unable to work and receives permanent disability. He is addicted to prescription painkillers. Mrs. Gomez has a steady job, but still they couldn't make ends meet. When they couldn't pay their rent and were evicted, Mrs. Gomez and the children entered an emergency shelter, but it accommodated only women and their children, not men, so her husband stayed with family and friends, moving from house to house. The staff at the emergency shelter helped the Gomezes find services for their seven-year-old daughter, who exhibited severe behavioral problems. After psychological evaluation and educational assessment, she was placed in special needs classes. The family next rented a house that was for sale but had to move on six months later when it was sold. They had no luck in finding an apartment; they were known for not paying their rent, and landlords refused to deal with them. A local church let them live in the church basement when they had nowhere else to go. They spent eight months there until the priest made a referral to a local emergency shelter. The family was accepted at the shelter and remained there for one year. The shelter staff helped the family obtain a federal rental subsidy. They moved to an apartment where they've been living for five years.

There remains much controversy within the social service field as to whether homeless families were at risk before they became homeless or are at risk because they are homeless. Yet whatever the reasoning, these families need support to cope with their homelessness as well as assistance when they secure permanent housing. A family-centered treatment approach is adaptable for work with these families, whether they are living in their car, a shelter or welfare motel, or newly found permanent housing. Each housing situation is characterized by its own treatment dilemmas.

A worker who receives a referral for a homeless family living in their car focuses on helping the family find a more appropriate place to stay. If the family is in a shelter or a welfare motel, the worker assists the family in locating permanent housing, completing applications for subsidized housing, and making sure the family's welfare benefits are not interrupted. (In some states, a family can lose benefits if they don't have a permanent address because the welfare department refuses to send checks to a temporary address.) Another problem for families living in a shelter concerns school. An immediate issue is how to transport a child to school. A more subtle one concerns the attitudes of school administrators and teachers. Teachers may be overwhelmed by the multiple problems many homeless children exhibit in the classroom. They may be resentful as well about having to address the problems when they prefer to focus on teaching. Such resentment may grow when they learn that the child is living in the community temporarily and was not previously a resident; the child may be considered an outsider who is placing a burden on the community. The child is often blamed or suffers as a result of this attitude. Educating school administrators and teachers about homelessness and developing a cooperative partnership is paramount.

A worker may be referred to a family who just obtained permanent housing, a situation with its own stresses. The family must become familiar with a new neighborhood, children must adjust to a new school, and the family, although relieved to have a permanent place to live, must adjust to their new living situation. During this time, they need support in learning how to live together again. In fact, it takes at least six months of support to keep the family from becoming homeless again.[34]

Meeting the family's concrete needs is a priority and will facilitate the formation of a trusting worker-family relationship. As in other situations, it is important to help the family recognize its own strengths. For instance, reminding the family that they are together and are working on solving the problem of their homelessness is essential. Pointing out the lack of affordable housing nationwide is often useful in helping them realize that they are not to blame for their homelessness. By encouraging the family to continue their struggle and demonstrating a belief in the family, the worker is helping the family to see themselves in a more positive way, enabling them to make choices and move toward changing their situation.

Coordinating services lessens the impact of homelessness on families. These families are typically involved with numerous service systems, which are often unaware of each other. Shelter staff, teachers, welfare workers, counselors, and others must meet regularly to ensure comprehensive service delivery.

Working with a homeless family can be very difficult, but the potential for a worker and family to see the results of their efforts is great. When a family finally locates permanent housing and children are enrolled in school, worker and family can see that something tangible has been accomplished. Once permanent housing is secured and the family is physically stabilized, the worker begins to assist the family with any internal issues they want to work on while addressing other unmet external needs, such as vocational training, jobs, or day care. The family and worker have built a trusting relationship that will be the basis for their future work together.

Family Reunification

A family-based treatment approach can be adapted to reuniting families just as it has been used to avert placement, but many children are reunited with their parents without the benefit of this sort of program. Without this resource, families usually encounter difficulty with the transition, and children are often placed again. In a study of sixty-two cases in which children reentered placement after an abortive attempt at family reunification, 90 percent of the families had an ongoing problem that remained unresolved at reunification.[35] Time and again, workers find that there is not enough emphasis placed on family reunification. It is frustrating for them to see children do well in placement and go home, only to be placed again later because there were no reunification services. Lack of reunification programs is also discouraging for families who want to get their children back but require intensive intervention. Services are typically provided during the transition period when a child is in placement and about to return home, but they need to be extended for a period of time *after* the child has returned home to ensure that the child is safe and to reinforce gains made during the child's transition from placement back home.

We need to reconceptualize our thinking about reunification, perhaps along the lines suggested by the authors of *Together Again: Family Reunification in Foster Care*. Rather than looking at reunification as an either/or proposition—either a total return home or a severing of parental rights—they propose that it "should be viewed as a continuum, with levels or outcomes ranging from full reentry into the family system, to partial reentry, to less extensive contact, such as visiting, phoning, writing, and other affirmations of the child's membership in the family."[36] When reconnecting a child, workers must consider not only biological parents but extended and foster families, as well as significant others. In states where open adoption is legalized, it may be in the best interests of the child to be cared for on a day-to-day basis by adoptive parents, with the biological family maintaining some type of contact, so that the child does not experience total separation and loss.

A new conceptualization of family reunification opens up a variety of options for both families and workers. Here, we discuss reunification in terms of a child's returning home since this presents the most difficulty for workers due to their concern for the safety of the child.

A number of family reunification models have developed around the country, most of which utilize intensive intervention for a prescribed length of time. But as we note throughout this book, zealously holding to preconceived models nullifies the philosophical underpinnings of family preservation. No one formula is effective across the board for all families. Instead, treatment interventions, intensity of services, and length of service delivery must be tailored to the unique needs of each family. Some families respond well to an intensive service over three to six months; others require intensive service for three months, move to having workers available on a weekly basis for three months, and then have workers available as needed over a six-month period.

The most important factor among the many to consider in making the decision to reunite abused or neglected children with their families is child safety. A worker must fully understand why the child was removed and what services are necessary to ensure the child's safety if placed at home again. This is not a one-time determination. The worker continually assesses the level of risk by examining family strengths and difficulties. Assessing level of risk is also useful in determining the intensity of services families will require following reunification. For example, if a family is reunited when the father is released from prison, having been incarcerated for sexually abusing his daughter, the worker will want to be in the home frequently, intensively, and over a significant period of time.

Reunification is a gradual, planned process that includes everyone involved with the family: siblings, extended family who play a significant role in the child's life, informal support systems like the church or a self-help group, foster care or residential placement, or other public agencies. The worker needs to work with the child's family and the foster family or residential staff to ensure that messages to the child are consistent, that parents are included in treatment decisions, and that no factors consciously or unconsciously undermine the reunification process.

A family-centered approach works well when applied to family reunification because it is practical and hands-on and emphasizes working from strengths. The family-based worker has a smaller caseload than most public child welfare workers and can devote the time and energy necessary to form a trusting relationship and partnership with parents. Parents who have had their children placed in residential or foster care often feel alienated and alone, and they may feel that the child welfare system is hostile and punishing. The worker acts as advocate and, once a trusting relationship is established, provides meaningful interventions to assist parents in reunification.

A family-based worker has the time to orchestrate, facilitate, and oversee frequent home visits by the child during the reunification process. Transporting a child to and from home visits can be time-consuming but is an important aspect of reunification. Moreover, time spent in the car enables the worker to prepare the child for the visit on the way to the family's home and to talk about the visit on the return trip.

This system works best when the worker meets with the family for a significant period of time (as much as six months) prior to reunification. Supervised visits with the child should occur at least two or three times a week. Concrete services as well as psychological support is provided to parents while the child is in placement, and parents will benefit by participating in a parent support group. As the child gets closer to returning home, visits become more frequent and longer. For example, instead of being together for two hours, the family is together for four hours. Instead of having two home visits a week, there are four weekly. Eventually the family spends an entire day together, then the child spends the night, then a weekend, and then a week.

Short home visits (e.g., one hour) fail to offer the worker a clear picture of a family's dynamics. Most families can behave well for an hour-long home visit. The more frequently a child visits and the longer the visits are, the more accurate and realistic a picture the worker gets of the family. It's important to determine how the family relates to each other: Do they play together? Do they sit down and eat meals together? Families often experience a honeymoon period when working toward reunification; the child and parents try to portray the perfect family in an attempt to show the worker and themselves that things can improve. Overnight visits with the worker present in the evening and first thing in the morning are helpful in facilitating a discussion among parents and children (the child and his or her siblings) about the positive aspects of the visit, disappointing aspects, and identification of issues on which the family needs to work.

Since the worker is in the home, he can provide immediate, concrete, and ongoing feedback to parents concerning their interaction with their child(ren). The worker can help parents develop new ways to play with and discipline their children by encouraging family communication through role modeling. The worker makes a habit of meeting with parents after the visit to process what happened and to plan for the next visit. This is also an excellent time to comment on improvements and to discuss any problem areas the worker or family may have observed.

The worker is available to provide ongoing assistance to the family once they have been reunited, for this is the time of greatest difficulty. Thus, it is crucial to ensure supportive services—ideally for six months to a year after the child has returned home, with at least weekly meetings and with parents continuing in a parent support group. Families will be thwarted in their reunification efforts until we invest the same time, money, and energy in reunification that we currently put into out-of-home placement.

7
Dealing with Diversity

F amily-based services must place greater emphasis on promoting services that respond to the diversity of clients. The concept of diversity must be expansive, encompassing culture, ethnicity, race, religion, gender, sexual orientation, class, and disability. Currently, the attention paid to these issues by family preservation programs varies considerably and is often haphazard.

Cultural Competency

Those who work with family-based services encounter families of diverse cultural and ethnic backgrounds. Since ethnicity is such an integral part of people's makeup and inextricably linked to who they are and how they live, professionals cannot afford to overlook or profess ignorance of their clients' cultures. The book, *Ethnicity and Family Therapy* profiles a panoply of ethnic groups, suggesting a framework within which to work with families by building on each culture's attributes. "Ethnicity remains a vital force in this country, a major form of group identification, and a major determinant of our family patterns and belief systems."[1]

Two major factors have contributed to our inattention to the provision of culturally sensitive services. Most important is that white administrators who determine the direction of service delivery do not consider cultural diversity a priority. A commitment to diversity entails an attempt (whenever possible) to match consumer families to staff by ethnicity, from the administrative to the worker level. The second factor is the myth of the melting-pot ideology. For years, workers believed that treatment tailored to intervene with European-American families would be equally beneficial to all families, regardless of their ethnic heritage. The basis for this belief was the melting-pot ideology, which posited that all cultures would be integrated and accepted within the dominant culture. This paradigm captured the experience of white European immigrants because their physical attributes enabled them to fit in. However, the notion of our society as a happy melting pot is both outdated and flawed and its failure for people of color has been acknowledged.

A number of factors have pushed the United States to struggle with the need to address ethnic and cultural issues. One of them is the nation's shifting demographics. In the past decade, the Latino and Hispanic population has increased by more than 50 percent and the number of Asian-Americans more than doubled, largely because of immigration.[2] By the year 2000, it is estimated that people of color will comprise 40 percent of the service delivery system.[3] Other factors are the trend toward a global economy and the shift away from assimilation to biculturalism, defined as the ability to adapt to the dominant culture while maintaining ties to one's own ethnic group. Biculturalism poses an inherent conflict given that one's cultural values may conflict with those of the dominant culture.

Exploring Our Own Feelings

All workers must continually examine their own beliefs about people from other cultures and how they affect their work with families. Often these beliefs are based not on knowledge but on myths, stereotypes, and preconceptions. Lack of understanding can create barriers to service delivery, "and each barrier could represent a lost opportunity to help."[4]

The first step in developing cultural awareness is to scrutinize our own feelings and beliefs about ethnic groups other than our own. Everyone who grows up in a society has racial and ethnic stereotypes. They may be conscious or unconscious, subtle or obvious. What's important is recognizing and acknowledging these stereotypes and biases.

Clinical assessment and treatment are inevitably affected by differences in race, ethnicity, and culture that may exist between the worker and the family. The outcome of treatment depends on the counselor's ability to address rather than avoid or be thwarted by racial and cultural issues. He or she must realize, when intervening in family relationships, that "family structures, ... are not simply personal arrangements among family members. They are manifestations of the values of the cultural group to which the family belongs."[5] Most workers will contend that they are not prejudiced or racist, yet many therapeutic interventions are culturally insensitive. For instance, working toward making the spousal relationship more equal in a Hispanic family would be a violation of their cultural norm and no doubt cause problems among family members. On the other hand, supporting cultural norms that are sexist may not be in the best interests of individual family members.

Despite all that has been written on various ethnic groups, we must continually remind ourselves that generalizations about each group are simply that—generalities—and we must guard against letting these generalities become stereotypes. Within the broad categories of culturally different groups there are, additionally, various subgroups, making it even more difficult to generalize about a particular ethnic or cultural group. For example, Hispanic-Americans can be Latino, Puerto Rican, Mexicano, or Cuban, among others. Asian-Americans are Japanese, Chinese, Filipino, Korean, Vietnamese, Cambodian, Asian Indians, and others. Although these groups are broadly categorized as Hispanic- or Asian-American, each subgroup is vastly different, and there are great variations within each subgroup, and, of course, each family. The length of time a family has lived in the United States and the amount of family members' exposure to the dominant culture contribute to its own make-up. Many studies identify alcoholism as a major problem among Native Americans, yet this does not mean that all Native Americans are alcoholics, and workers must be vigilant not to bring this stereotype when assessing a Native American family.

Rather than making assumptions, counselors can ask families how they want their ethnic heritage identified. For example, some individuals would rather be called "La Raza" (the race) or "Latino" than "Hispanic." Similarly, African-Americans may prefer to be called "black" or "Americans of African heritage." Native Americans may prefer to be called "American Indians." What may be regarded as derogatory by one person may be considered an expression of racial pride by another.

It is impractical to expect workers to know everything about every ethnic group's values and beliefs. More important, workers must closely and continually examine and be attuned to their own prejudices. That is, they need to know more about themselves than their clients.[6] In addition, it is highly recommended that workers at least obtain a basic understanding of the minority groups within their geographic area.

Stigma, Racism, and a History of Oppression

The power and influence of the dominant culture cannot be overlooked because "those who control power and opportunity are often blind to fairness."[7] European-Americans represent the dominant culture in the United States, and their values and beliefs are reflected in traditional mental health counseling. These values not only clash with those of minority cultures but have also harmed these groups and reinforced oppression of them.

We can neither ignore that racism is on the rise in the United States nor dismiss the fact that "the world view of the culturally different is ultimately linked to the historical and current experiences of racism and oppression in the United States."[8] Many people are wary about seeing a counselor of a different race or culture. This skepticism has often been viewed by professionals as pathological, but it should instead be considered a strength based on the reality of the prejudice and discrimination that some groups have faced. Their long history with stigma, racism, and oppression is part of who they are and the context in which they have lived. This history is addressed as part of treatment. Counselors must openly acknowledge they're from a different ethnic group from their client.[9]

Studies show that certain ethnic groups not only underuse conventional mental health services but are also inclined to terminate counseling prematurely.[10] Many claim that culturally biased and insensitive treatment yields this result. No one can deny that most social service agencies utilize culturally biased assessment tools. Most of them are in English, but English is a second language for many clients. Even the way we define health and pathology is biased against ethnic groups. Although the Diagnostic and Statistical Manual of Psychiatric Disorders (DSM III-R), the diagnostic tool used by practitioners, emphasizes that "none of the current diagnostic classifications address the impact of race, ethnicity, or culture on the manifestation of symptoms and behaviors that suggest emotional difficulties," in fact, ethnic minorities disproportionately get the more severe diagnoses. In addition, clinicians and writers point out that many psychological problems originate from or are exacerbated by both environmental and social stressors—for example, unemployment, housing, health care, violence, and discrimination.[11]

Additionally, most research and media attention has emphasized the problems and pathology of ethnic groups rather than focusing, as family-based services do, on strengths and coping skills. All ethnic groups have unique strengths; the more a counselor can learn and the more the family can teach the counselor about their ethnic background, the stronger and more effective the counselor-family partnership will be.

Ethnicity plays a critical role in determining how people seek assistance. Certain cultural norms discourage seeking outside help. Perhaps stigma, shame, and discomfort are associated with counseling. Many individuals find support in their extended family and turn to them first for assistance. Asians do, for example; obtaining outside assistance such as counseling goes against the culture so counseling can be considered a disgrace to one's family.[12] Other ethnic groups may seek assistance but not from a public agency. African-Americans may look to the church and Native Americans to a native healer. Spirituality, important to Native Americans and Hispanics as a source of support, is typically overlooked by the mainstream culture. Asians, Puerto Ricans, and Greeks may complain of physical symptoms when under psychological stress and seek treatment for their physical problems.

Recent immigrants to the United States who come from countries characterized by widespread governmental corruption and oppression have a legitimate fear of government agencies based on their history. When a state child welfare worker pays a visit to a family to investigate a report of child abuse, it would not be surprising to find a family that fears the government agency has come to take away a family member. The worker who is simply trying to learn more about the family may be met by resistance because the family is anxious about divulging information they believe could be held against them. They may be fearful of jeopardizing their citizenship or even their lives.

Language and Communication Styles

Language is of key importance in working with families from different countries. It is, of course, beneficial if the worker speaks the family's native language, but that is not enough; the worker must understand and respect a family's values and culture as well. Many individuals from various ethnic groups can speak English and do so when they're away from home, but if they "do not use their native tongue in counseling, many aspects of their emotional experience may not be available for treatment."[13] (Perhaps all Americans should work toward becoming bilingual, instead of limiting themselves to speaking only English, assuming that ethnic groups will learn English.)

Even if a family speaks English as their native language, their dialect may deviate from the norm. A well-known example is "black English." An insensitive counselor may assume that a speaker using this dialect is uneducated because the grammar differs from that of standard English. If he corrects the speaker, the counseling relationship may suffer. The counselor should accept a person's language as part of his or her culture and not try to standardize it.

Besides language, there are more subtle differences in communication between minority groups and the dominant culture. One of the most common relates to eye contact. European-Americans consider eye contact a form of respect and a means of conveying honesty, and this white cultural norm (and bias) has found its way into counseling theory and practice. A client who fails to make eye contact may be viewed as disrespectful, dishonest, and avoiding or disagreeing with whatever point is being discussed. Yet many ethnic groups—Japanese-American, Mexican-American, and some Alaskan native groups—view eye contact as a sign of disrespect of authority. A counselor who misinterprets can gain a wrong impression of the family and negatively influence the course of treatment.

The authors of *Counseling the Culturally Different* observe that "many minority group individuals find the one-to-one in-office type of counseling very formal, removed, and alien."[14] Family-based services that provide in-home counseling respond to the uneasiness that individuals from certain cultures experience with traditional counseling. "To many culturally different people who stress friendship as a precondition to self-disclosure, the counseling process seems utterly inappropriate and absurd. After all, how is it possible to develop a friendship with brief contacts once a week?"[15] Explaining to families what to expect from the counseling process can allay their fears and anxiety since they often have misconceptions or are unfamiliar with counseling. Studies have indicated that preparing clients for what to expect in counseling influences successful treatment outcomes. A family-centered approach that advocates participating in activities with the family rather than simply using talk therapy can help put people at ease and foster a good counselor-family partnership. Home-based, family-centered services that stress the importance of developing a relationship are well suited to working with culturally different families.

Brisbane and Womble's *Working with African Americans* is highly useful; it contains numerous practical strategies that are eminently applicable to family-based work. One approach in particular is especially helpful: the use of abstractions. The authors maintain that African-Americans tend to terminate treatment if it is more distressing than their problem. Direct and continuous questions, personal questions, and a reliance on talk therapy may alienate them, particularly if the worker is not of the same race or culture.[16] When the counselor approaches problems abstractly, the individuals can personalize their own experiences, sharing as little or as much as they feel comfortable. The authors suggest using exercises, films, or quotations to provoke discussion, maintaining that this technique works especially well in group treatment for African-Americans but is also applicable to parenting, adolescent, and other groups. It can also be modified for use with individuals and families and is adaptable and useful with other ethnic groups, for example, Asian-Americans who do not readily divulge personal problems to strangers (the counselor), do not respond to ongoing questions, and consider suppression of strong emotions a cultural value. Approaching problems indirectly by using abstractions can create a less threatening environment and enhance the trust and rapport between the counselor and family.

Family-centered programs that sponsor support groups are acknowledging that many culturally different individuals feel more comfortable in informal settings—a church, a neighborhood community center, or someone's home. If families come to the program site, it's important that the agency display posters of people of color, or have magazines which emphasize people of color. When calling an agency in New York City that works with African Americans, callers placed on hold listen to rap music. Nuances such as these convey a message to culturally different individuals to take pride in their diversity.

Child Rearing

Every culture has its own family values concerning child rearing. There are vast differences among cultures in parental expectations and attitudes (the term "parents" refers to those who assume parental responsibilities) regarding child development. The European-American culture, for example, has delineated specific developmental milestones to which many parents rigidly adhere. Mexican families, on the other hand, have a more casual attitude, are less concerned about the attainment of developmental milestones, and are more accepting of their child's individualism.[17] What may be considered positive child-rearing behavior in one culture may not be in another. For example, a worker providing services to a Native American family noticed the parents didn't seem very excited about the birth of their first child and was concerned that they would be unable to bond with their baby. When the worker asked if they had wanted this baby, both parents seemed confused by the question. This worker did not know that Native Americans believe that gushing over a child is believed to endanger him or her.

Discipline practices vary from culture to culture. For example, Native American parents "rarely discipline their children unless real danger exists, believing that a child should be allowed to make mistakes and learn the natural consequences of misbehavior," whereas Puerto Ricans view "corporal punishment, if not excessive," as a valid disciplinary approach.[18] Styles of discipline also vary among cultures. For example, European-Americans believe in confronting problems head on; Asians tend to address problems indirectly in an effort to avoid conflict and ensure family harmony.[19] In disciplining their children, Asians use indirectness, deflection, and shame instead of direct confrontation.

Given the importance of extended family in many minority cultures, the worker needs to determine what roles family members play in regard to parenting and who has ultimate authority even when a child's parents are present. It could be that the grandmother, not the mother, is the decision maker. If grandparents or significant others play a role in parenting, they must be involved in determining how children will be disciplined. Their participation ensures consistency and encourages those assuming parental functions to work together. Involving extended family in child rearing and discipline can offer concrete as well as emotional support.

Extended Family and Informal Helping Networks

Families from most ethnic groups place considerable importance on the family, but their definition of "family" is not the same as that of the American culture, which uses "family" to refer to the nuclear family. Family structures vary greatly around the world; thus, "family" has a different meaning to different people and must be defined by the client. The extended family, for example, "is the basic system in which African Americans have their emotional, physical, spiritual, social, and nurturing needs met." Family means relative-kin (blood relatives) and social-kin (nonblood relatives). Thus, friends are "adopted" and treated as if they are related and are called "aunt," "uncle," and so forth.[20] "African Americans are very relationship-oriented; the ability to bond and support each other (extended families) has been a survival mechanism since slavery."[21] The Asian culture, which stresses the family over the individual, is diametrically different from Western culture, which promotes individualism and independence as a valued treatment goal.

A counselor may erroneously consider a client to be overly involved with his or her family without realizing that this assessment is based on Western, not Asian, cultural norms. Most Native Americans grow up in extended families and are raised by relatives living in separate households who have parental functions. In this culture, cousins are considered siblings. Like the Asians, Native Americans believe that family and tribe are more important than the individual. For Hispanics, the family is salient, and loyalty runs strong. Extended family often encompasses nonblood relatives such as godparents. Like African-Americans, Hispanics typically seek advice from their extended family and friends before turning to traditional services.

Family-based workers acknowledge and respect the importance of the extended family, recognizing it as a significant source of strength and support. The worker appreciates the interdependence within the extended family and builds on this rather than rigidly adhering to Western values that emphasize encouraging autonomy and independence from one's family of origin. In the African-American culture "grandparents assist with the socialization of children. Not only do parents expect this, but grandparents themselves expect to play a central role in the lives of their grandchildren."[22] A study of one Native American tribe revealed that more than 90 percent of grandparents residing in separate households played a central role in the lives of their children and grandchildren, participating in their day-to-day upbringing.[23] Respect for elders is paramount in many ethnic groups; Westerners fail to recognize the importance of elders.

The emphasis in family-based systems on linking families with natural support systems is well suited to minority families, who often turn to extended family, churches, and indigenous healers for advice and support. Staff can "mobilize these informal networks and natural support systems for their clients, . . . identifying community leaders who are natural helpers and utilizing them as brokers between the formal and informal treatment systems."[24] Given the strong spiritual orientation of certain ethnic groups, it is not uncommon for spiritual leaders to become vital allies in the treatment process.[25] For example, spiritualism, important to the Hispanic culture, can be incorporated in the therapeutic experience. A mental health center in New York City has spiritualists participate in sessions with family therapists in an effort to help the family better deal with a crisis. Including individuals significant to a family's culture in the treatment process often proves beneficial.

Future Directions

Although the literature on cross-cultural issues has increased dramatically, this knowledge for the most part has failed to reach practitioners. Knowledge about other cultures must be translated into practical skills and become an integral part of treatment. Cultural diversity is not a core part of university curricula and is not viewed as integral to professional training. Typically in human services, crises are addressed first, and other issues, like cultural competency, that do not appear pressing often get lost. We must build incentives to promote the development of cross-cultural competency; for example, public agencies must mandate contracted agencies to devise plans to move toward cultural competency or make professional licensure contingent on obtaining cross-cultural training. Higher education, both undergraduate and graduate, needs to address issues of cultural competency, making cultural courses mandatory instead of elective, and incorporate cultural diversity into the social work curriculum, particularly in child welfare. Generalizations about various ethnic groups can guide our work; however, we must not lose sight of the fact that treatment is not based upon a framework of generalities but is highly individualized.

Sexual Orientation

Society should embrace any family configuration that is healthy. This includes acknowledging and valuing gay and lesbian life-styles.

Institutional Heterosexism and Homophobia

Like individuals of different cultures, gays and lesbians have a history of institutional oppression. Institutional heterosexism, for example, is a supposition by those who run institutions (including social service agencies) "that heterosexuality is in all ways better than homosexuality. It can be as blatant as refusing to provide services to [gay and] lesbian clients or as subtle as assuming that all clients are heterosexual."[26]

Institutional oppression is evident in many major cities in the form of referendums that determine whether gay and lesbian rights are protected. Legal issues, especially, illustrate institutional oppression. When heterosexuals have children, laws protecting their families exist. A nonbiological gay or lesbian parent has no legal status, unless he or she adopts the child. Every state denies gay and lesbian couples the legal benefits of marriage; two states actually prohibit gays and lesbians from adopting children[27]; and some states forbid homosexuals from becoming foster parents.

One of the most pressing issues gays and lesbians often face is the possibility of losing child custody through divorce. Some judges consider gay and lesbian parents unfit by virtue of their sexual orientation. This has ramifications for providing home-based work. If a parent is involved in a custody battle or divorced and worried that the biological parent may sue for custody, it is not uncommon for this parent to keep his or her sexual orientation a secret. The worker's goal to establish a relationship with a family can thus be thwarted by a gay or lesbian parent who fears facing severe consequences by revealing his or her sexuality. "There are many awkward moments for lesbian and gay parents and they must constantly weigh the value of privacy with the courage to tell the truth."[28] Getting involved in a culture of hiding and secrecy is the antithesis of empowerment, trust, and respect, salient goals of family-centered work. Since treatment entails encouraging people to give up their secrets, in this case, the worker is in a clinical double bind: whether to encourage parents to be honest with their children or risk losing custody.

Same-sex couples are fighting for the same basic civil rights that hetero-sexual couples often take for granted. Something as seemingly simple as attending a parent/teacher meeting is complicated by whether only the bio-logical mother or both mothers should attend. Being gay or lesbian has *real* risks, forcing gays and lesbians to be constantly vigilant about their actions. Children from gay and lesbian families repeatedly claim that most of the pressure they suffer growing up has to do with society's expectations, not their families. "Ignorance, insensitivity, stereotyped thinking, outright prej-udice, discrimination, and a host of negative attitudes all can be loosely grouped under the umbrella of homophobia."[29]

It wasn't until 1969 that the Stonewall riot, an impromptu protest pro-voked by a police raid of a gay and lesbian bar in Greenwich Village, began the struggle for gay and lesbian civil rights in the United States. As a result, many gays and lesbians came out of the closet. In 1973, the American Psy-chiatric Association removed homosexuality from its Diagnostic and Statis-tical Manual of Psychiatric Disorders (DSM II). No longer could gays and lesbians be classified as pathological because of their sexual orientation. ". . . while homosexuality was depathologized, therapists were given no guidance as to how to think about or work with their gay and lesbian clients."[30]

Twenty years later, professionals are still struggling to provide sensitive services, yet there remains little guidance from the literature or academia. Like racism, homophobia often elicits strong feelings. No worker wants to be thought of as prejudiced, yet too often workers fail to explore their own feelings about homosexuality. Most heterosexual workers fall somewhere along a continuum between two extremes. At one end are heterosexual work-ers who may ignore or underestimate the differences between themselves and gay and lesbian clients, treating them like everyone else. At the other end are heterosexual workers who try to conceptualize all problems in a gay or les-bian client's life as revolving around this individual's difficulty accepting his or her sexual orientation.[31]

An example of the problem of homophobia is illustrated in the case of Mrs. Chandler, a fifty year old grandmother who had custody of Tricia, her four year old granddaughter, because her daughter was drug-involved. A male worker from the state child welfare agency had been monitoring Mrs. Chandler's ability to parent and he repeatedly made derogatory remarks to her. When the worker quit his job, he was replaced by a female who referred the family to a home-based program because she expressed concern about Mrs. Chandler's ability to parent. Although neither worker had spoken to

Mrs. Chandler openly about her lesbian lifestyle, both included this in their reports. Although nothing had been said directly to Mrs. Chandler, she believed that the state agency had been hostile to her. After negative experiences with the two state workers, it was hard at first for Mrs. Chandler to trust Sue, the home-based worker.

Sue's visits often found Mrs. Chandler and her lover together, yet Sue did not discuss their relationship. It was not even clear whether Mrs. Chandler and her lover lived together. Eventually, however, Mrs. Chandler learned to trust Sue enough to talk about her relationship of five years and their plans to buy a house together. Sue viewed the family as stable, with Mrs. Chandler setting appropriate structure and being responsive to Tricia's needs. In addition, Tricia's comfort around her grandmother's lover was apparent.

Gay and Lesbian Parenting

There are three- to eight-million gay and lesbian parents in the United States raising six- to fourteen-million children.[32] Most of them had their children during heterosexual marriages. Included are a variety of family types: some include a single parent and children; some have a live-in partner who is a co-parent and may or may not have his or her own children; others have a partner who does not live with the family; some also include ex-lovers who are part of the family. They all face such issues as whether to live alone to avoid stigmatizing the children, how much of a co-parent the gay or lesbian parent should be, and how much the children should be told.[33]

Sexual orientation becomes a treatment issue when the behaviors of the adults in the household adversely affect the growth and development of a child. For example, Mrs. Karp, twenty-seven, was a single parent lesbian raising her four year old son, Bill. Mrs. Karp had pictures of women making love tacked to the walls of both her bathroom and her bedroom. Whether heterosexual or lesbian, it is inappropriate to expose a young child to such pictures. The worker's intervention entailed educating Mrs. Karp about creating appropriate boundaries.

With most families, issues such as race and class are evident whereas sexual orientation is not. One way to initially assess sexual orientation is to ask a single parent if anyone is co-parenting the child. This open-ended question leaves room for responses such as an ex-husband or ex-wife, boyfriend or girlfriend, or gay or lesbian partner. A worker may need to know this information if a treatment goal is to improve parenting. What are the roles in the family? Who sets the rules and enforces the consequences—the biological parent, the co-parent, or both? These issues are analogous to those dealt with in families in which there is a new step-parent, yet societal stigma and homophobia further complicate matters in gay and lesbian families.

Gay and lesbian parents are inventing a new model of relationship, developing their own rules and roles for their family. Same-sex parents are

"creating a culture of [their] own, evolving new definitions of family relationships. . . . Even under the most severe persecution, our spirits have pre-
vailed. We have learned to make our differentness our strength."[34] In
addition to defining their relationship, same-sex parents must deal with many
issues that heterosexual parents never even consider. This can be as basic as
what a child will call his or her two fathers to distinguish between them. Or
it can be as complex as how to deal with one's family of origin when coming
out or finding a day care center that values different family constellations.
Gay and lesbian couples experience stress from different systems simultaneously, including their families of origin, their own relationships, the gay
and lesbian community, their religious community, and mainstream society.
All of these complicating factors make creating a family a challenge.[35]

Individual developmental issues play a role in the family life-cycle. Although some gays and lesbians may acknowledge their sexual orientation,
others may require assistance in developing a positive gay or lesbian identity.
The coming out process can be framed as a developmental issue.[36] It is not
uncommon to find that one partner in a couple is comfortable with people
knowing he or she is gay or lesbian whereas the other is not. If this disparity
creates problems for the family, part of the worker's role may be addressing
these issues.

Effects on Children

Teenagers face numerous stresses whether they grow up in gay and lesbian
families or grow up thinking they have heterosexual parents only to learn
that their parents are getting divorced and that one parent is gay. This often
creates a disruption in the family and is particularly difficult for teenagers
struggling with their own identities and peer acceptance. Adolescents are
likely to experience anger or confusion about a parent's sexual orientation.
Some go to great lengths to keep their parent's sexuality a secret. Many go
through a stage when they're worried that they're going to be gay. On a
positive note, some youngsters claim that growing up in a gay family has
made them more accepting of people's differences and helped them understand oppression.

Families in which a Child is Gay or Lesbian

Gay and lesbian teenagers face an especially difficult transition to adulthood.
Due to their stigmatized minority status, they are at high risk for running
away from home, truancy, substance abuse, prostitution, HIV/AIDS, and
suicide. Societal stigma and the internalization of homophobia, difficult
enough for adults, are found by adolescents to be overwhelming. Families of
lesbian and gay youth may react with denial, fear, or anger in response to
their child's sexual orientation. The worker helps these families acknowledge

their child's sexual orientation and cope with the societal stigma that accompanies having a gay or lesbian child.

The LaPlante family was referred to a family-based program because Jennifer, fifteen, had repeatedly run away from home. She had been acting out in school and was often truant. At their first family meeting, Jennifer said she had a crush on her female teacher who was her mentor. Jennifer's parents responded with disbelief. (Had Jennifer had a crush on a male teacher, this would have been considered normal.) The worker told the parents that their daughter was going through a developmental stage and that it is not uncommon for teenagers to struggle with their sexual identity.

The worker met with Jennifer's teacher who felt very nervous and uncomfortable about Jennifer having a crush on her. The worker suggested that they meet with Jennifer. She prepared the teacher for this meeting. The teacher clearly told Jennifer that her feelings were not reciprocal and that teacher/student relationships were inappropriate. She also advised Jennifer to put her feelings aside so that they wouldn't interfere with her schoolwork.

A month later, Jennifer revealed that she had had a sexual relationship with a female teenager and her parents responded with shock and anger. The worker encouraged them to talk about their feelings. They said that they knew nothing about homosexuality. After the parents calmed down, the worker suggested that they might find it helpful to talk to parents who had lesbian children.

Gay and Lesbian Community Resources

A worker's familiarity with resources in the gay community is critical. Resources may include gay and lesbian parent support groups, gays and lesbians of color support groups, twelve-step programs for recovering gay and lesbian substance abusers, and shelters for battered lesbians. Children of gays and lesbians may find support in a group specifically for them. There are also support groups for gay and lesbian teenagers. A familiarity with legal matters as they relate to gay and lesbian families is essential for workers, e.g. an understanding of guardianship, wills, health care proxies, and durable powers of attorney.

8
Staff

P rogram success hinges on the quality of direct care staff, the most critical resource of family preservation programs. Recruiting, selecting, supervising and training home-based counselors differ from that of typical social service programs because the job of a family-based counselor is difficult and often more stressful than office-based treatment. Programs require well-developed screening and selection procedures to ensure that staff have the right blend of skills, experience, and personal characteristics. If a program is part of a larger agency, it must develop its own hiring procedures. This chapter examines a number of issues about staff, from important qualities to worker safety.

Staff Qualities

Home-based family-centered programs have had great difficulty recruiting qualified staff. Since academic training in family preservation is scarce, workers are often unprepared for this field. Job advertisements typically reap resumés from individuals trained in individually oriented social work practice or in family therapy, not family preservation. Those new to the field may not realize what is entailed in working with high-risk families and quit shortly after they begin.

It takes a certain kind of person to do this work, necessitating a unique combination of personality traits, experience, and expertise. Educational degrees should not be emphasized. More relevant to this work is one's life experience, as well as attitudes, beliefs, values, and skills to do the work. Unlike traditional counseling programs, home-based programs place a strong emphasis on the importance of personal qualities when hiring staff.

Workers are selected based on the following qualities:

- Their commitment to biological families as being the best place for children as long as they are safe.

101

- Personal traits: sensitivity, compassion, flexibility, creativity, high energy, ability to establish rapport, willingness for growth, and a good sense of humor.

- Strong interpersonal communication skills, common sense, maturity, good judgment, persistence, and patience.

- Experience or interest in learning a family systems approach using an empowerment model that focuses on strengths, recognizes cultural competencies, and utilizes an array of interventions instead of relying on a single approach.

- Willingness to meet families' concrete needs and provide case management services, as well as offering therapeutic interventions.

- Ability to develop collaborative working relationships with agency colleagues, private and state agencies, and informal community resources.

- Ability to work well in an unstructured work environment, including a willingness to work flexible hours, which often means being on-call.

- Ability to adjust to the demands of family-based work and simultaneously set clear boundaries between work and personal life.

- Ability to be comfortable in the homes of families with different values, life-styles and cultures.

The interview process provides an opportunity to determine a potential employee's attitudes, values, and skills. What is the interviewee's attitude toward high-risk families? Does he conceptualize systemically as opposed to individually? Does he think of himself as an expert or as a learner? Role playing a variety of situations during the interview will quickly reveal the interviewee's attitudes and abilities. So will discussing an array of hypothetical situations a counselor may come across.

Workers operate from a generalist instead of a specialized framework. They are equipped and willing to deal with multiple problems, knowing that they can rely on their peers, supervisors, or community resources for assistance. Since education in family preservation is scant, programs often have no choice but to hire staff with outpatient family therapy experience. These individuals learn to adapt their skills, or develop new skills, when working with families in their homes. Staff recognize the importance of collaborating and allying with families as well as community resources.

Maturity, good judgment, and good instincts are characteristics to look for in staff. One of the inherent dangers of this work is the tendency of staff to let their job become their life. Staff need to be able to set clear boundaries between themselves and their clients, recognizing that they have lives of their own and have ways to get their needs met outside of work.

Staff Supervision and Training

Extensive individual and group supervision as well as ongoing in-house and external training are integral to the success of family preservation programs. Programs ensure a nurturing and inspiring environment for growth through supervision and staff training. Management acknowledges that the most important work is done by direct care, not managerial staff. A supportive, collegial work environment characterized by good relationships between management and staff is a necessity. Staff supervision and training provide education, support, and nurturance and serve as a vehicle through which to build an esprit de corps, imperative for staff who need to know that they can count on each other. High morale and teamwork is especially critical when working with high-risk families.

Programs offer extensive supervision, typically weekly individual supervision, peer supervision through clinical groups, and supervision in families' homes. Each type offers advantages. Individual supervision is personal and tailored to meet the needs of each staff person. Group supervision offers staff a chance to learn from peers, providing an excellent opportunity for role playing and peer support. In-home supervision of workers is particularly useful because the supervisor can get to know the family and can provide immediate feedback on the counselor's work. Supervisors are available to counselors twenty-four hours a day to assist during a crisis. They are critical when tough decisions must be made.

For counselors who work alone and don't have daily contact with their peers, supervision is essential for maintaining objectivity and getting support as well as feedback. This is particularly critical in cases of sexual abuse and domestic violence, which can be highly stressful and often traumatizing for workers. In home-based, family-centered work, it is imperative to have an experienced supervisor who is both approachable and available. Counselors must feel comfortable with their supervisors and be assured that they are accessible in a crisis.

Supervisors must have leadership skills. Rather than tell their supervisees what direction they need to go in, supervisors follow the lead of their supervisees, moving at their pace. They relate to workers in the same way that workers are expected to relate to families, supporting and modeling family preservation values and philosophy. They recognize, acknowledge, and build on the strengths of their staff. Like workers, they too require ongoing support and training from management.

A family-based program offers a well-planned, rigorous staff training program consisting of orientation, skill building, role playing, and case presentation, with an emphasis on challenging populations. Certain in-house training is mandatory to ensure that workers operate from the same philosophical framework and have a grasp of basic issues. Mandatory training includes tools for building a relationship with families, as well as practical, hands-on techniques on working from strengths. This approach of working with strengths may seem elementary or self-evident but is "fundamentally different" from that of traditional helping models, and staff may need special training.[1] In-house training is provided on an ongoing basis, with staff input on training topics. In addition, workers are encouraged to attend workshops to improve their skills.

Referring workers and others involved with the program's families are given an orientation to the program and invited to participate in future in-house training to ensure that they understand what the program offers and the populations it can best serve. This also creates a forum for program staff and involved workers to get to know each other. Invitations to participate in case consultations are also extended. The program's goal is to encourage positive working relationships between program staff and other workers involved with families, based on the belief that an ecological approach is optimal for families.

It is essential that family-based programs recruit trainers who possess specific expertise in family-based services rather than only family therapy. This is too seldom the case. Because of a scarcity of trainers, family-based programs are too often forced to rely on family therapists, who have not worked with high-risk families, have not provided home-based services, and are unfamiliar with the values, principles, and philosophical underpinnings of the family preservation movement. Thus, the presentations they make may be irrelevant, dealing with middle-class families who come to office-based sessions once a week, or failing to address the critical problems that characterize high-risk families, such as substance abuse, domestic violence, or sexual abuse. As the family preservation movement develops, and trainers with experience and expertise in home-based family services are recruited, programs will decrease their reliance on family therapists unfamiliar with this type of work.

Collaborating with Academia

There needs to be more collaboration between academia and family preservation programs in regard to staff recruitment, education, and training. One of the critical needs is for the development of undergraduate and graduate programs in family preservation, as well as the creation of continuing education for family-based workers, so that family-based programs can find qualified staff. Although academia has responded on a small scale, much remains to be accomplished.

Only a handful of colleges and universities offer courses in family preservation. Typically adjunct faculty teach these courses, and when they leave the courses are no longer taught. The few academic institutions that offer a family preservation specialization do so only at the graduate level. The availability of undergraduate courses would fill a growing need since many programs employ bachelor-level staff. Since most schools of social work have a child welfare concentration, family preservation courses could be easily integrated in that curricula.

Social work training actually contradicts the philosophy of family preservation by insisting on building artificial barriers between the worker and family. For example, social work training may teach students never to disclose information about their personal lives; giving out one's home telephone number to families is usually considered completely unacceptable. In addition, social work training is typically based on a deficit-driven, as opposed to strengths-focused, model with office-based treatment. When counselors fresh out of school begin working with high-risk families, they often find that their training has failed to prepare them for this type of work that requires a reliance not on technique but on instinct.

Preventing Burnout

The program director sets the tone of the program. This person monitors counselors' caseloads, sets realistic expectations, ensures ongoing staff supervision and training, and encourages staff to maintain a balance between their personal and professional lives. Some program directors, however, have an unstated but understood expectation that staff will devote their lives to the program. Clearly this is both an unrealistic and unhealthy norm, encouraging and setting the stage for burnout.

Working with high-risk families is stressful. Counselors need help to maintain their objectivity, lessen stress, and obviate burnout. Unless they deal with their anger and stress, they will be unable to give much to families. Workers require some outlet for their stress and cannot feel as if they are all alone with families' problems.

Burnout prevention begins by ensuring that staff feel that their work is appreciated and recognized and can include any of the following suggestions:

- Providing mandatory stress management training, especially for newly hired workers.
- Involving staff in decision making and seeking their opinions about program development, indicating that management respects and values their opinions. Involvement encourages personal investment in the program and enhances staff commitment.
- Offering good salaries, good employee benefits (e.g., long vacations or "flex" time), and opportunities for promotion.
- Ensuring regularly scheduled individual and group clinical supervision, as well as backup supervision in crisis situations.

- Holding regular meetings to share information, providing ongoing continuing education, and special events for staff such as an annual retreat, annual picnic, or a volleyball team that plays regularly. Some events are work related; others are just plain fun. Both build staff morale and encourage camaraderie.

- Creating opportunities for staff to grow professionally by encouraging them to present at conferences, provide inservice training for their colleagues, publish articles on family-based services, collaborate with academia to offer courses or do research on family-based services, and provide consultation and training to other agencies.

- Recognizing staff achievements both formally and informally.

Educating Other Professionals

Home-based work is still considered somewhat out of the mainstream. It is not uncommon for family-based workers to find that family preservation is met with resistance and skepticism by most other professionals, who have little understanding and typically no training in working with families in their homes. Home-based family-centered programs housed in traditional settings, such as child welfare agencies, mental health centers, and psychiatric hospitals, often encounter difficulty from other agency staff for three reasons. First, other professionals may resent the lower caseloads and flexible hours of home-based staff. Obviously home-based staff do not work a typical 9-to-5 workday, and since their job necessitates working nights, staff are not regularly seen at the agency. Staff from other programs may question why home-based staff are infrequently at the office. Second, office-based staff usually see clients once a week for one hour, typically working from a deficit-driven model in which diagnosis is critical. They may be completely unfamiliar with the philosophy behind family preservation and the importance of working from a strengths-focused model. Many may never have entered the homes of their clients. Third, home-based work is not deemed as professional or as respectable as office work. These issues are often unspoken or subtle, yet they do exist.

There are a few single-purpose agencies solely providing home-based services. These organizations were designed with a single mission in mind, with a management committed to the philosophical underpinnings of home-based family work. Contrast this with a larger agency with many diverse programs in which management may be unfamiliar with the values and philosophy of home-based work. A lack of management expertise and understanding can thwart the efforts of home-based staff and impose barriers to effective service. If a home-based program is housed in a multiservice agency, the program's uniqueness must be acknowledged and addressed.

Developing a Multidisciplinary, Culturally Competent Staff

Many programs place an emphasis on the development of a multidisciplinary or transdisciplinary staff. There are two ways to go about this. One is to hire people from varied disciplines with varied degrees—perhaps a nurse, a psychologist, a social worker, and an occupational therapist who work in changing teams of two, pairing together based on the needs of the family. More and more programs are finding value in having a nurse on staff to address families' health-related issues. In fact, visiting nurse programs are adapting family preservation principles, a natural fit since these programs have a history of working with families in their homes. The second way is to hire staff with similar degrees but with varied expertise. If a team approach is employed, staff with diverse expertise can team together. If an individual approach is employed, the family's counselor may bring in another staff person to assist as needed or may seek the staff person's advice without having him or her meet with the family.

Since few universities offer training in cultural competency, programs must train their staff to work with people of different races, cultures, classes, religions, and family constellations. (The Department of Social Work at New Mexico State University is an exception, offering a culturally sensitive family preservation curriculum and publishing excellent documents on the subject.) Developing cultural competency does not mean offering a series of trainings; it is a commitment made by management over a long period of time. Traditional service delivery approaches have historically been insensitive to cultural issues, leaving minority children more vulnerable to out-of-home placement as a result of cultural bias and oppression. Staff who are unfamiliar with different cultural and ethnic groups and who are unable to communicate with a family because they can't speak the family's language need to overcome these barriers.

Home-based programs in geographic areas with large minority populations recruit minority staff. The Lower East Side Family Union in New York City recruits bilingual staff from the same ethnic backgrounds as those in the neighborhoods they serve; many are from that same neighborhood. Staff from diverse cultural backgrounds serve as a resource for nonminority staff.

Sometimes a home-based program requires assistance in working with a family of a particular culture. Staff in a home-based program with a caseload that was three-quarters Hispanic found themselves at a loss when a Turkish family was referred. Since no one on staff had expertise with this culture, an interpreter was hired to help the worker communicate with the family and understand the family's culture and customs. A rarely discussed dilemma often faced by home-based programs in multicultural communities is the difficulty of always having someone on call who can speak the diverse languages of the clients served.

Professional and Paraprofessional Staff

The educational qualifications of workers vary widely across programs. Some programs insist on workers with degrees, others employ paraprofessionals, and some have professionals and paraprofessionals work together as a team. Professionals who work with high-risk families possess diverse skills. Their training enables them to quickly recognize family patterns that paraprofessionals may not as readily notice. They are able to maintain boundaries and understand a variety of treatment techniques from which to draw upon.

Paraprofessionals, also known as family support workers, community workers, mental health workers, or parent aides, are a vital and powerful resource in the delivery of social services, especially when working with high-risk families. Many families quickly develop a special bond with paraprofessionals because they have faced similar problems; they also tend to view "these visitors [as] less threatening and more easily accepted than more highly trained persons who shared fewer common experiences with their clients."[2] Paraprofessionals serve as role models. Families look up to paraprofessionals because they have succeeded and give families hope that change is possible. Often paraprofessionals are from the same neighborhoods or ethnic backgrounds, making it easier for families to develop relationships. As a result of their own experiences, paraprofessionals are adept at accessing community resources, obviating the bureaucratic responses that prohibit service to those who cannot comprehend intricate and complex procedures. Paraprofessionals commiserate with families about the difficulties of dealing with bureaucracies while walking families through the process.

Although the advantages of employing paraprofessional staff are numerous, there are also drawbacks. Paraprofessionals may become overinvolved and overidentified with families, requiring close supervision regarding boundary issues. Paraprofessionals must recognize that they cannot be everything to the families they serve, and they should not because the philosophy of family preservation is to help people learn how to help themselves.

Employment of paraprofessionals is often an excuse for underpayment and sexism, since most are women. It is distressing that the strengths of paraprofessionals are often overlooked, minimized, or criticized. In programs that team a paraprofessional with a professional, hierarchical problems are not uncommon. Additionally, a frequent problem is that the family is more comfortable with the paraprofessional, and a wedge is driven between team members.

Individual and Team Approaches

In some programs, staff work individually with families; others employ a team approach; still others use an individual or team approach based on the family's needs.

An individual approach has certain advantages. Considering a high-risk family's distrust of social workers and history of negative involvement with the social service system, it is often easier and less intrusive for a family to develop a relationship with one rather than two workers. In addition, a family is more likely to develop rapport with a worker who provides concrete as well as therapeutic services. The ongoing communication and coordination between team members is time-consuming and expensive, making an individual approach more economical.

There are many different types of team approaches. Some programs have team members split the responsibilities. If a clinician (professional) and a family worker (paraprofessional) work as a team, the clinician provides counseling and case management, links families with resources, and supervises the family worker, while the family worker offers day-to-day assistance with the children and the household. Another program uses an interdisciplinary team made up of a nurse, occupational therapist, and psychologist. Yet another variation is to assign a primary and secondary worker to each family, with the primary worker responsible for providing direct service and coordinating resources and the secondary worker serving as a back up in the event of an emergency. The secondary worker and the family know each other and can work together if the primary worker becomes unavailable.

There are numerous advantages to a team approach.

- Team members provide extra support to the family and also encourage and support each other, minimizing stress and burnout. The likelihood of being overwhelmed by and becoming enmeshed in a family is reduced, and objectivity is enhanced because a team member can provide feedback.

- If one team member has problems working with a family member, another team member can assist.

- If a team member is ill, on vacation, or leaves the job, emergency coverage and treatment continuity are ensured because the family has an established relationship with the other team member(s).

- Team members serve as role models, demonstrating to the family how people can work together to resolve problems. Team members can assume complementary roles with the family (e.g., nurturing versus confrontational). Having a male and female on the team demonstrates how the sexes can negotiate problems.

- Programs working with a particular ethnic group can use a team comprised of one member that is of the same race or ethnicity as the family. This arrangement helps the family develop a trusting relationship while encouraging them to develop a relationship with someone who is not of the same ethnic group.

- Through a team approach, changes accomplished in family meetings can be supported through additional work with individual family members and subsystems. For example, it may prove useful to work with the parents and children separately, or it may be useful to meet with a teenager individually.

- A team approach diminishes the extent to which a family can become dependent on one worker, enabling the family to develop more than one trusting relationship.

- Safety of workers is enhanced since workers go to homes together.

A team approach also has disadvantages. A team's competency is dependent on each counselor's ability to work cooperatively toward the same goals, not allowing conflict and competition to divide them. A team approach can be fraught with logistical problems; team members must not only coordinate family meeting times but must also meet regularly to plan and discuss family treatment.

There is no empirical evidence to indicate that either an individual or team approach is more effective. Instead of searching for the answer to this question, it seems more important to ask for what types of families an individual or team approach is more effective.

Worker Safety

Workers must ensure their own safety. Safety concerns vary across programs, but there are some basic guidelines applicable to all staff.

1. Use common sense. Trust your intuition, if you feel unsafe, for whatever reason, you probably are unsafe and should do whatever is necessary to protect yourself.

2. Become familiar with the neighborhoods you enter so that you'll know each area (e.g., know the safest place to park).

3. Give someone your schedule. If you're going to a dangerous neighborhood, call in when you return. A number of home-based programs use portable phones or car phones, particularly in rural areas or high-risk urban areas.

4. Keep enough gas in your car and keep your car in good condition to ensure you don't break down in the middle of nowhere, or in a dangerous urban area.

5. If, during a home visit, drug use, drug dealing, or violence (or the threat of it) occurs, leave immediately if you feel endangered.

9
Where Do We Go From Here?

A Call for Systems Reform

In 1990, the U.S. Advisory Board on Child Abuse and Neglect claimed that "child abuse and neglect in the United States now represents a national emergency."[1] In their 1993 report, this group called for immediate attention to this emergency. Numerous publications emphasize not only a national child abuse crisis but point to the devastating failure of our whole service system to serve children and their families.[2] Many factors contribute to the calamitous condition of families in our nation: family problems are more severe, parental substance abuse continues to escalate, the number of infants and very young children entering foster care is increasing, child poverty is expanding, and juvenile courts are placing more youngsters. Ten percent of American children—6 million youngsters—live apart from their parents.[3]

The good news is that legislators, federal and state governments, foundations, and private agencies are finally speaking the same language. They have acknowledged that "although the problems and risks experienced by disadvantaged children are often multiple and interrelated, the responsibility for addressing these problems is usually lodged in so many agencies and systems that services are inevitably fragmented and no single organization is accountable."[4] They have also recognized the crying need for comprehensive system reform, with a continuum of noncategorical, family-focused services, ranging from family support through family preservation.

A federal bill for family support and family preservation finally passed in the summer of 1993. The Omnibus Budget Reconciliation Act of 1993 (PL 103-66) includes nearly $1 billion over five years for family support, preservation, and reunification programs. Funds were also included for evaluation, research, training, and technical assistance. The heretofore autonomous constituencies of family support and family preservation must unite to share and build on their experience and expertise. Although the two movements developed separately, they must come together to create a continuum of preventive and supportive services. "When communities are able to offer a pyramid

111

of assistance that matches the pyramid of family needs, problems are likely to be solved or alleviated at earlier stages, when they are easier and less costly to address."[5] Together family support and family preservation services can influence family policy, service delivery, and research.

A family-centered approach is a conceptual framework within which to assess and intervene with families regardless of whether children remain in their homes, foster care, residential placement, or institutions. We must radically alter the paradigm we have relied on to work with children, with the goal of universalizing a family-focused approach and providing comprehensive, coordinated, strengths-focused services. Family support, preservation, and reunification must become a permanent part of each state's service continuum. Traditionally, family preservation has been associated with the child welfare system. We must make family-centered programs available statewide across all service systems, promoting cross-system planning and implementation.

Social Programs Are Not Enough

Families are experiencing severe stress as a result of a depressed economy; and undermining of social supports; increases in poverty, unemployment, homelessness, drug and alcohol abuse, AIDS, violence, and crime; faltering educational systems; and lack of affordable health care. A faltering economy has wreaked havoc on families, and a lack of informal support systems, such as extended families and neighbors, has exacerbated the stress families feel. Neighborhoods have grown increasingly violent, dangerous, and tense. Family-based programs alone cannot reverse these catastrophic national trends; they are not a panacea. Surely, "only the naive or irresponsible would blame major social problems on social service failures or claim that social services reform will eliminate poverty or social pathology."[6] No matter how good family-based programs are, they serve only a small percentage of families involved with public agencies and cannot be expected to rectify the complex problems confronting families today. Instead, there must be "a unified national commitment to alleviating the underlying causes of poverty, homelessness, violence, and our other social afflictions."[7]

The first change that must happen to reverse this nation's downward spiral is a transformation of our values and priorities. This will take time and prove a considerable undertaking, but we have no choice but to pursue this course, and we must begin now. "The pandemic violence, poverty, racism, and child neglect in America are all symptoms of the loss of spiritual anchors in our nation."[8] The American culture has sent a message, whether inadvertently or deliberately, that violence, racism, and poverty will be tolerated. Not only have we relinquished our values of decency and respect, and lost hope for the future, but it feels as if there is nothing we can count on. We must radically change this cultural message, rethinking our priorities and rebuilding our values. We must validate the importance of the family. "That sense of belonging is what we must recapture across the nation."[9] A critical part of changing values and priorities entails an immediate need to acknowledge and address cultural oppression in our society, making a genuine, concerted commitment and effort to promote multiculturalism. This necessitates a federal, state, neighborhood, and personal commitment.

The second important change is to address larger social issues, garnering government commitment to strengthen families. This calls for a close examination of the impact of current and proposed government policies to determine if policies are supportive or hostile to families. Further, we need to believe in and fund prevention, not just pay it lip-service. Failing to offer early preventive support, we provide a costly infusion of services that often come too late to be effective. This approach has proved an inexorable failure.

Finally, we must balance the need to provide direct service with involvement in strengthening the neighborhoods and communities in which families live. We cannot work with families in a bubble; we must work with them within the context of their environment. This necessitates that family support and preservation programs play some role in the community, addressing underlying problems of poverty, drugs, and violence, "thereby integrating community organization activities with family support and family preservation services."[10] We must return to the settlement house perspective, improving the communities in which families live. As workers, we have a unique perspective in that we encounter problems that can best be addressed on a systems or community level; we must play an active role.

Program Evaluation: What Is Success?

Program development is far ahead of program evaluation. Demonstration projects with large evaluation budgets often conduct research; however, smaller programs, representing the bulk of family-based programs, typically lack funding to evaluate their services. If they do evaluate, there is no systematic way of sharing these findings with the field. These unpublished drafts are usually shelved.

There is far too little interaction among programs, policy, and research. We must acknowledge the importance of research and ensure that research findings play a role in program development. Research studies are often isolated events that fail to reach programs and influence service delivery. Fortunately, recent federal legislation allocates funding for evaluation and research, which we hope will improve service provision. In addition to evaluating family preservation services, there should be equivalent evaluation of foster care and other child welfare services.

It is astounding to consider how family preservation has caught on and spread like wildfire without being substantiated by research confirming its efficacy. Despite the Clark Foundation's emphatic nationwide promotion of Homebuilders, its own publication, *For Children's Sake: The Promise of Family Preservation,* cautions that "there is not yet proof—using an academically acceptable, experimental design—that family preservation can decrease the number of placements."[11] Further, the very underpinnings on which Homebuilders is based are called into question in a book supported by the Clark Foundation pointing to the lack of theory and research about intervening at the point of crisis and providing time-limited service. "There is no forceful theoretical or evaluative argument for drawing on crisis theory or crisis intervention constructs to boost the helpfulness of IFPS [intensive family preservation services]." In addition, "the theory and evidence in support of lasting effects of brief interventions is not persuasive."[12] The promulgation of a single model in the absence of theory and research is cause for concern.

We must determine which program components as well as which length and intensity of service work best for what types of families. "Until this information is obtained, we will not know why our programs are successful and we will have no hard data on which to base the development of future programs."[13] Most important, we must redefine success. Traditionally placement prevention has been the primary, and sometimes the only, measure of success. Yet it seems unrealistic to shoot for 100 percent placement prevention with the implication that any placement is deemed a failure. No other programs are held to such a stringent, rigid definition of success. This goal sets up out-of-home placement as a failure when it may be in the best interests of the child to be placed; this does not always preclude reunification. Also, we must define placement: Does it mean respite? living with relatives? going to foster care or a residential program? There are variations regarding type and length of placement; simply determining whether a child has been placed offers limited information. One family-based program reported being penalized by its funding source for hospitalizing referred clients because the funding source maintained that hospitalizations (placement) could occur under no circumstances. This is a negative and dangerous side effect of equating placement prevention with success. Moreover, it potentially jeopardizes the safety of the identified client, family members, and others. Clearly, placement prevention cannot be inextricably linked to success.

The only way to evaluate placement prevention is to determine whether a child is at imminent risk of placement. This determination is made by individuals at referring agencies or by a screening committee, not by family preservation programs. Assessment of imminent risk is subjective, and "it also appears that caseworkers steer families with children at grave risk directly into foster placement."[14] If workers strongly believe that a child should be placed, it is unlikely that they will refer the family to family-based services.

Many family preservation programs are lax about determining whether a child is at imminent risk of placement; their goal is providing services to families, and they are not as concerned with criteria for placement. In their report on California family preservation programs, Yuan and her coauthors "strongly cautioned that imminent risk is difficult to define, difficult to determine, and difficult to implement."[15]

Since preventing placement has been the criterion for referral to many family preservation programs, discussion about whether it is actually possible to target children at imminent risk is critical. Assessment of imminent risk of placement has become a standard on which to base research, yet "a recent review of the research on family preservation suggests . . . that given the difficulties of operationalizing imminent risk and in predicting future placement, these be abandoned as referral criteria and measures of outcome."[16] In a conference presentation, Schuerman, Rzepnicki, Littell, and Budde pointed out that the most important question facing the family preservation field is the issue of targeting. They believe "it is unlikely that . . . [family preservation] services will have a substantial direct effect on overall placement rates or on the numbers of children in substitute care, although particular approaches with particular kinds of clients may be effective in reducing the likelihood of placement."[17]

Evaluating programs based on imminent risk of placement pits family preservation against out-of-home care. Family preservation advocates have polarized out-of-home services by selling family preservation as placement prevention. The field must rethink its position, considering ways to incorporate family-based services with out-of-home care. Although a seemingly commendable goal, substituting other outcome measures for placement prevention is likely to meet with resistance from advocates who believe that they can sell the model as cost-effective only if it does, in fact, prevent placement.

Program evaluation often focuses on child outcomes rather than changes in family systems. Evaluations must be expanded to measure changes in family dynamics and in the interaction between the family and the community. "Little attention has been paid to modeling the interaction of . . . ecological variables such as the level of community impoverishment, level of stressful life events impinging on the family and the level of social support experienced by family members."[18] We must evaluate family-based programs within an ecological context. Evaluation needs to mirror treatment, measuring success from a systems perspective.

There is a need for longitudinal research as well. Evaluations must be long term if we are to determine whether family gains are sustained. Many programs limit evaluation to the families' involvement in the program, and others follow families for only six months to one year. For programs that refer families to follow-up services (especially short-term intensive programs), we must assess and delineate the impact of family preservation services independent of the effect of follow-up services, in an effort to determine which interventions are tied to having an effect on the family.

Since the new federal legislation (PL 103-66) has set money aside for evaluation and research, perhaps this will encourage the family support and family preservation movements to work together as they try to come to terms with evaluation issues. Despite the commonalities between the two movements, each movement is, for the most part, familiar only with its own research studies. It would be worthwhile for them to exchange ideas and share information.

The Need for a Consumer-Driven Service System

We need to place greater emphasis on cultural competency in curricula, ongoing training, and programs themselves. We must base the design of assessment strategies and treatment interventions on the ethnicity and culture of our clients and become sensitive to issues of sexual orientation and class.

Although family preservation emphasizes the importance of forming partnerships with families and highlights the need for consumer feedback, there needs to be much more import placed on consumer involvement. The family preservation movement can benefit from the work of the Child and Adolescent Service System Program (CASSP), a federally funded program that assists states and communities in developing community-based systems of care for severely emotionally disturbed youngsters and their families. The model system of care and principles of service delivery promoted by CASSP are consonant with the philosophy of family preservation. CASSP promotes strong consumer involvement. Family preservation needs to practice what it preaches. We tell families that they have many strengths and that they are valuable. We must now make consumer involvement a priority. We need consumers on the board of directors of our national organizations, such as the National Association for Family-Based Services, and private agencies with family-based programs. Families can play an active role, helping to design and improve programs to make them more responsive to clients. In addition, we must more extensively solicit families' input in our evaluations to determine the efficacy of our work. Families can quickly tell us what worked and what didn't, yet we often neglect to collect families' opinions, analyze them as a whole, and use this information to improve interventions. We must hire former clients as staff in our programs. We also need to hold conferences that bring together family members, service providers, policymakers, advocates, and researchers. The Research and Training Center at Portland State University (see the Resource Directory for further information), an organization focusing on family support and children's mental health, can serve as a role model for consumer involvement.

Beware of Pitfalls . . .

As a burgeoning field, there is much that family preservation must beware of. Like other movements, it is susceptible to conventionalism. Already there is talk of standardization. When a movement grows, people develop different conceptualizations. This diversity is readily apparent in a number of areas. The family preservation movement is comprised of diverse advocacy organizations and numerous program models. Organizations have developed different frameworks for classifying family preservation models; for example, the National Resource Center for Family Based Services and the Child Welfare League of America each has its own classification framework. Diversity is also evidenced by the variety of existent program models.

The field of family preservation has become distracted, embroiled in controversy over the definition of family preservation and quibbling about which program model is best. We have lost sight of our mission. This divisiveness is sapping our energy, preventing us from focusing on pressing issues. Getting caught up in jargon and definition is petty and can only do the field a disservice. Just as we encourage diversity in regard to cultural issues and intervention strategies, so must we recognize and embrace the importance of diversity of program models. Rigidly promoting a specific model is contradictory to the philosophical underpinnings of family preservation, not to mention that it overlooks the unique needs of each family. The values and philosophy of diverse family preservation models have many similarities; we must focus on what unites us instead of arguing over what divides us.

We must worry about total conformity. There is a push to standardize the field by ensuring that the definition of family preservation is synonymous with the short-term intensive program model. This is already happening; many new to the field are led to believe that there is only one model since it is the most widely publicized. The heavy financial backing behind Homebuilders is responsible for its infiltration of the child welfare system and its dramatic national impact. Despite the money behind this short-term intensive model, there remains a vocal minority that calls for diversity. We must beware of this push for homogenization and instead celebrate our differences.

Family preservation is characterized by its creativity and energy. The more mainstream or institutionalized the movement becomes, the more the danger of being co-opted. "When the revolutionaries or the reformers succeed and power is acquired, the emphasis on change is lost as, ironically and paradoxically the new guard assumes the mantle of power and inevitably becomes the status quo."[19] We must guard against professionalism if it means forfeiting the authenticity, sincerity, and informality that are hallmarks of family preservation. It could also mean the proliferation of specialization, which brings with it jealousy and division among different disciplines, each defending their own particular niche. Can family preservation continue to retain and reflect its unique philosophy without being swallowed up in the mainstream?

Resource Directory

Center for the Study of Social Policy, 1250 Eye Street, NW, Suite 503, Washington, D.C. 20005. (202) 371-1565. Publications and newsletter on family preservation.

Child and Adolescent Service System Program (CASSP) Technical Assistance Center, Center for Child Health and Mental Health Policy, Georgetown University Child Development Center, 3800 Reservoir Road, NW, Washington, D.C. 20007. (202) 687-8635. Publications focusing on family work with emotionally disturbed children and adolescents and their families that can generalize to work with other populations. Key publication: *Toward a Culturally Competent System of Care.* 2 vols., 1989 and 1991.

Child Welfare League of America, Family Preservation Project, 440 First Street, NW, Suite 310, Washington, D.C. 20001-2085. (202) 638-2952. Publications on family preservation.

Children's Defense Fund, 25 E Street, NW, Washington, D.C. 20001. (202) 628-8787. Publishes a newsletter, *CDF Reports,* and other publications.

Clearinghouse on Child Abuse and Neglect Information, P.O. Box 1182, Washington, D.C. 20013. (800) 394-3366 or (703) 385-7565. Offers literature on child abuse and neglect.

Community Program Innovations, P.O. Box 2066, Danvers, Massachusetts 01923-5066. (508) 774-0815. Publishes a newsletter and provides training and consultation nationally to agencies working with high-risk families.

Domestic Abuse Project, 204 West Franklin Avenue, Minneapolis, Minnesota 55404. (612) 874-7063. Publishes a newsletter, *Domestic Abuse Project Research Update,* and other publications on domestic violence. Also holds conferences.

Edna McConnell Clark Foundation, Office of Communications, 250 Park Avenue, New York, New York 10017-0026. (212) 986-7050. Publications on family preservation.

Family Resource Coalition, 200 South Michigan Avenue, Suite 1520, Chicago, Illinois 60604-2404. (312) 341-0990. Publishes a newsletter, *Family Resource Coalition Report,* and other publications, and sponsors conferences.

Family Service Association of America, 44 East 23d Street, New York, New York 10010. (212) 674-6100. Publishes journals and books.

Family Violence and Sexual Assault Institute, 1310 Clinic Drive, Tyler, Texas 75701. (903) 595-6600. Publishes a newsletter.

Federation of Parents and Friends of Lesbians and Gays, 1012 14th Street, NW, Suite 700, Washington, D.C. 20005. (202) 638-4200. This national organization provides support groups and public education to families through 200 local chapters and hotlines in the United States, Canada, and six other countries. It also offers training and publications for professionals concerning the needs of gay and lesbian youth.

Gay & Lesbian Parents Coalition International, P.O. Box 50360, Washington, D.C. 20091. (202) 583-8029. Publishes books and a newsletter and holds conferences.

National Association for Family-Based Services, P.O. Box 005, Riverdale, Illinois 60627. (319) 396-4829. Publishes *NAFBS Newsletter* and sponsors conferences.

National Center for Children in Poverty, Columbia University School of Public Health, 154 Haven Avenue, New York, New York 10032. (212) 927-9162. Publishes a newsletter and other publications on children in poverty.

National Center for Clinical Infant Programs, 2000 14th Street North, Suite 380, Arlington, Virginia 22201-2500. (703) 528-4300. Publishes a newsletter, *Zero to Three,* focusing on infants and toddlers, as well as other publications, and holds conferences.

National Center on Women and Family Law, 799 Broadway, Room 402, New York, New York 10003. (212) 674-8200. Publishes a newsletter, literature on domestic violence, and public education materials.

National Clearinghouse Against Domestic Violence, P.O. Box 34103, Washington, D.C. 20043-4103. (202) 638-6388. Offers literature on domestic violence.

National Clearinghouse for the Defense of Battered Women, 125 South 9th Street, Suite 302, Philadelphia, Pennsylvania 19107. (215) 351-0010. Publishes a newsletter, *Double-Time,* as well as other publications on domestic violence.

National Council on Family Relations, 1910 West County Road B, Suite 147, St. Paul, Minnesota 55113. (612) 633-6933. Publishes a newsletter, journal, and books.

National Resource Center on Family Based Services, School of Social Work, University of Iowa, 112 North Hall, Iowa City, Iowa 55242. (319) 335-2200. Publishes a newsletter, *Prevention Report,* and other publications and provides training and consultation nationally.

National Victims Resource Center/NCJRS, Dept. AIF, P.O. Box 6000, Rockville, Maryland 20850. (800) 627-6872 or (301) 251-5525 or 5519. Provides victim-related information to practitioners, policymakers, researchers, and crime victims. Free and low-cost materials.

Research and Training Center for Children's Mental Health, Florida Mental Health Institute, 13301 Bruce B. Downs Boulevard, Tampa, Florida 33612-3899. (813) 974-4661. Publishes a newsletter, *Update,* focusing on mental health services for children and their families. Also publishes other publications and holds conferences.

Research and Training Center, Regional Research Institute for Human Services, Portland State University, P.O. Box 751, Portland, Oregon 97207-0751. (503) 725-4040. Publishes a newsletter, *Focal Point,* and other publications focusing on children with emotional disabilities and their families.

Notes

Introduction

1. U.S. Government Accounting Office, 1993, p. 36.
2. Children's Defense Fund, 1992, p. ix.
3. Tollett, 1993, p. 8.
4. McGoldrick, Pearce, and Giordano, 1982, p. xv.
5. Child Welfare League of America, 1993b, p. 4.

Chapter 1: The Family Preservation Movement

1. Levine and Levine, 1992, p. 44.
2. Birt, 1956; Compton, 1962, 1979a, 1979b; Overton, 1978.
3. Overton et al., 1959, clarifies the philosophical principles on which family-centered programs are based today. This book not only provides a useful overview of the St. Paul program but is just as relevant today.

A number of other research and treatment projects were undertaken based on the Family Centered Project of St. Paul. See Geismar 1971b; Geismar and Krisberg 1967; and Geismar and LaSorte 1964. It is unfortunate that individuals designing and staffing family-based programs today tend to ignore the important work accomplished by these early projects.

4. Allen, Brown, and Finlay, 1992.
5. A number of authors stress the importance of assessing the family

within the many systems with which it interfaces. See Alexander, 1974; Aponte, 1976a, 1976b, 1977; Auerswald, 1968, 1972; Carter and McGoldrick, 1980; Compton, 1979b; Gatti and Colman, 1976; Geismar, 1971a; Geismar and Krisberg, 1967; Hartman and Laird, 1983; Hoffman and Long, 1969; Janzen and Harris, 1980; Lloyd and Bryce, 1984; Mannino and Shore, 1972; Meyerstein, 1977; Minuchin, 1970a, 1970b; Orcott, 1977; Powell, 1980; Taylor and Carithers, 1976; Umbarger, 1972; Woodbury and Woodbury, 1969.

6. Kaplan, 1986a.

7. Howard, 1992.

8. Warsh, Maluccio, and Pine, 1993, p. 10.

9. Patterson, 1992, p. 6.

10. Children's Defense Fund, 1992.

11. Flaherty, 1993, p. 3.

12. Most of these statutes were approved in the late 1980s. Barthel, 1992b.

13. Telephone conversation with Marcia Allen, Executive Director, National Resource Center on Family Based Services, March 19, 1993.

Chapter 2: Family Preservation

1. Maybanks and Bryce, 1979.

2. Friedman, 1993; Nelson, Landsman, and Deutelbaum, 1990; Ronnau and Sallee, 1992; Sandau-Beckler, 1993; Sudia, 1993a; Warsh, Maluccio, and Pine, 1993.

3. Ronnau and Sallee, 1992, p. 3.

4. Sudia, 1993a.

5. Stein-Cowan, 1992.

6. Barthel, 1992b.

7. Sallee and Mannes, 1992, p. 9.

8. Barthel, 1992a, 1992b; Bowlby, 1983; Bryce, 1981; Goldstein, Freud, and Solnit, 1973, 1979; Kagan, 1991; Littner, 1967; Lloyd and Bryce, 1984; Markowitz, 1992a; Minuchin, 1970a; Morton and Grigsby, 1993; Stone and Stone, 1983; Wolock et al., 1979.

9. Children's Defense Fund, 1992.

10. Sallee and Mannes, 1991b.

11. Children's Defense Fund, 1992.

12. Hancock and Pelton, 1989; Hodges and Blythe, 1992; Holbrook, 1983; Overton et al., 1978; Wasik, Bryant, and Lyons, 1990; Woods, 1988.

13. Telephone conversation with Marcia Allen, Executive Director, National Resource Center on Family Based Services, March 19, 1993.

14. Kamerman and Kahn, 1989a; Zalenski, 1993.

15. Allen and Zalenski, 1993.

16. Simon, 1984.

17. U.S. General Accounting Office, 1993, p. 32.
18. Yuan, 1992, p. 7.

Chapter 3: High-Risk Families and Interfacing Agencies

1. Overton, et al., 1978, p. 6.
2. Aponte, 1976b, p. 433.
3. Kamerman and Kahn, 1989a, pp. 9–10.
4. Ibid.
5. Ibid., p. xiv.
6. Ibid., pp. 59–60.
7. Allen, Brown, and Finlay, 1992; Birt, 1956; Brown, 1968; Buell et al., 1952; Children's Defense Fund, 1992; Geismar and LaSorte, 1964; Jacobi, 1968; Kamerman and Kahn, 1989a; Kaplan, 1986a.
8. Auerswald, 1972; Compton, 1979b; Hoffman and Long, 1969; Jacobi, 1968; Janzen and Harris, 1980; Kaplan, 1986a; King and Rabinowitz, 1965; Mannino and Shore, 1972; Meyerstein, 1977; Minuchin, 1970a; Overton et al., 1978; Sallee and Mannes, 1991b; Selig, 1976.
9. Kamerman and Kahn, 1989a, pp. 170–171.
10. Ibid.
11. Children's Defense Fund, 1992.
12. Zalenski, 1993.
13. Telephone conversation with Dr. Jessica Segré, October 1992.

Chapter 4: A Framework for Beginning Family Work

1. Segré, 1993, p. 2.
2. Overton et al., 1978, p. 15.
3. Lloyd and Bryce, 1984, p. 120.
4. For further reading on genograms and ecomaps, see Hartman and Laird, 1983.
5. For further reading, see Carter and McGoldrick, 1980, 1989.

Chapter 5: Treatment Strategies

1. Barthel, 1992a, 1992b; Chilman, 1966; Clark, Zalis, and Sacco, 1982; Geismar and Krisberg, 1967; Halper and Jones, 1981; Kaplan, 1986a; McKinney, 1970; Rabin, Sens, and Rosenbaum, 1982; Wasik, Bryant, and Lyons, 1990.
2. Barthel, 1992a, 1992b; Fraser and Haapala, 1987–1988; Morton and Grigsby, 1993.
3. Maslow, 1954.

4. Geismar, 1971b; Jones, 1976; Jones, Magura, and Shyne, 1981; Jones, Newman, and Shyne, 1976.

5. Baldauf, 1993; Beck and Jones, 1973; Bryce, 1981; Carter and McGoldrick, 1980; Compton, 1979b; Geismar, 1971b; Geismar and Krisberg, 1967; Halper and Jones, 1981; Hollis and Wood, 1981; Hutchinson, 1983; Janzen and Harris, 1980; Jones, Magura, and Shyne, 1981; Jones, Newman, and Shyne, 1976; Kaplan, 1986a; Lawder, Poulin, and Andrews, 1984; Lloyd and Bryce, 1984; Rabin, Sens, and Rosenbaum, 1982; Ronnau, 1990; Stroul, 1988; Wasik, Bryant, and Lyons, 1990.

6. Wasik, Bryant, and Lyons, 1990, p. 155.

7. Lloyd and Bryce, 1984, p. 61.

8. Wasik, Bryant, and Lyons, 1990, p. 15.

9. Goldstein, Freud, and Solnit, 1973; Kaplan, 1986a; Lloyd and Bryce, 1984; Wasik, Bryant, and Lyons, 1990.

10. Stein-Cowan, 1992.

11. Sallee and Mannes, 1991b, p. 23.

12. Massachusetts Department of Social Services, 1993, p. 7.

13. Dunst, Trivette, and Deal, 1988.

14. Stein-Cowan, 1992.

15. Lloyd and Bryce, 1984.

16. This example was suggested by Chad Morse, who was born and raised in Alaska.

17. Stroul, 1988, p. 18.

18. Lloyd and Bryce, 1984.

19. Overton et al., 1978, p. 128.

20. Epstein and Shainline, 1974; Goldstein, 1973; Halper and Jones, 1981; Janzen and Harris, 1980; McKinney, 1970; Morse et al., 1977; Taylor, 1972; Taylor and Carithers, 1976; Thorman, 1982.

21. Shure and Spivack, 1972, 1978; Spivack, Platt, and Shure, 1976; Spivack and Shure, 1974.

22. Gesimar, 1971b; Giblin and Callard, 1980; Janzen and Harris, 1980; Jones, Magura, and Shyne, 1981; Jones, Neuman, and Shyne, 1976; Kamerman and Kahn, 1989a; Orcott, 1977.

23. Friedman, 1993, p. 7.

24. Auerswald, 1968, 1972; Carter and McGoldrick, 1980; Halper and Jones, 1981; Heying, 1985; Hoffman and Long, 1969; Lloyd and Bryce, 1984; Mannino and Shore, 1972; Maybanks and Bryce, 1979; Umbarger, 1972; Warsh, Maluccio, and Pine, 1993.

25. Whittaker, Kinney, Tracy, and Booth, 1990, p. 106.

26. Carter and McGoldrick, 1980; Friedman, 1993; Minuchin, 1974; Minuchin et al., 1967.

27. Whittaker, Kinney, Tracy, and Booth, 1990, p. 93.

28. Alexander, 1973, 1974; Alexander and Parsons, 1973; Kaplan,

1986a; Minuchin, 1974; Minuchin and Montalvo, 1967; Minuchin et al., 1967; Parsons and Alexander, 1973; Satir, 1967.

29. Sue and Sue, 1990.

30. Alexander, 1973, 1974; Alexander and Parsons, 1973; Bryce and Lloyd, 1981; Cautley, 1979; Kaplan, 1986a; Lloyd and Bryce, 1984; Parsons and Alexander, 1973; Stroul, 1988; Wasik, Bryant, and Lyons, 1990; Whittaker, Kinney, Tracy, and Booth, 1990.

31. Glasser, 1965.

32. Berg, 1992, p. 13.

33. For further reading on solution-oriented therapy, see Berg, 1992; Berg and Miller, 1992; de Shazer, 1984, 1985, 1988, 1991; Friedman and Fanger, 1991; O'Hanlon and Weiner-Davis, 1989.

Chapter 6: Special Issues in High-Risk Families

1. Moss, 1993.

2. U.S. Department of Health and Human Services, 1992.

3. Ibid., p. 6.

4. This case example was suggested by Dr. Eric Emery, San Francisco Family Institute, 1993.

5. Barnes, Chabon, and Hertzberg, 1974, p. 609.

6. See Letich, 1992; Vanderbilt, 1992.

7. Denise Gelinas, "Family Therapy: Characteristic Family Constellation and Basic Therapeutic Stance" in Sgroi, 1992; Lanning, 1992.

8. Letich, 1992; Vanderbilt, 1992.

9. Barrett and Trepper, 1992, p. 45.

10. Mowrer, 1987, p. 2.

11. Telephone conversation with Kevin Creeden, August 30, 1993.

12. Gelinas, "Family Therapy," in Sgroi, 1989, p. 25.

13. Ibid.

14. Barrett and Trepper, 1992.

15. Madanes, 1990.

16. Vanderbilt, 1992.

17. Ibid., p. 63.

18. Telephone conversation with Kevin Creeden, August 30, 1993.

19. National Coalition Against Domestic Violence, n.d.; Straus, Gelles, and Steinmetz, 1980.

20. Stark and Flitcraft, 1988, p. 101.

21. Wasik, Bryant, and Lyons, 1990.

22. George, 1990, p. 5.

23. U.S. Department of Health and Human Services, 1992; Gordon, 1988.

24. Children's Defense Fund, 1991.

25. Wegscheider, 1981.

26. National Institute on Drug Abuse, 1987.

27. Anita Septimus, "Caring for HIV-Infected Children and Their Families: Psychosocial Ramifications," in Anderson, 1990, p. 103.

28. Mary G. Boland, "Supporting Families Caring for Children with HIV Infection," in Anderson, 1990; conversation with Michael Cook, September 1993.

29. Kübler-Ross, 1975.

30. Children's Defense Fund, 1991, 1992.

31. Ibid., 1992, p. 38.

32. Kozol, 1988.

33. Bassuk, Rubin, and Lauriat, 1986, p. 1100.

34. Waxman and Reyes, 1987.

35. National Association of Social Workers, 1993.

36. Pine, Warsh, and Maluccio, 1993, p. 6.

Chapter 7: Dealing with Diversity

1. McGoldrick, Pearce, and Giordano, 1982, p. 3.

2. Issacs and Benjamin, 1991.

3. Cross et al., 1989.

4. Issacs and Benjamin, 1991, p. v.

5. McGoldrick, Pearce, and Giordano, 1982, p. xiii.

6. Brisbane and Womble, 1992.

7. Ibid., p. xxii.

8. Sue and Sue, 1990, p. 5.

9. Brisbane and Womble, 1992, suggest questions to ask that will bring up the subject of race and color. They also address the importance of letting clients define their class.

10. Sue and Sue, 1990.

11. Issacs and Benjamin, 1991, p. 19.

12. Sue and Sue, 1990.

13. Ibid., p. 46.

14. Ibid., p. 28.

15. Ibid., p. 40.

16. Brisbane and Womble, 1992.

17. McGoldrick, Pearce, and Giordano, 1982.

18. Locke, 1992, pp. 53, 151.

19. Sue and Sue, 1990.

20. Brisbane and Womble, 1992, p. 1.

21. Issacs and Benjamin, 1991, p. 112.

22. Harrison, 1993, p. 24.

23. Sue and Sue, 1990.

24. Issacs and Benjamin, 1991, pp. 33–34.

25. Brisbane and Womble, 1992; Hill, 1993; Issacs and Benjamin, 1991.

26. Geraldine Faria, "Educating Students for Family-Based Practice with Lesbian Families," in National Association of Family-Based Services, 1992, p. 19.

27. Martin, 1993.

28. Laster, 1992, p. 10.

29. Markowitz, 1991, p. 29.

30. Ibid., p. 28.

31. Ibid.

32. Martin, 1993.

33. Falco, 1991.

34. Martin, 1993, p. 6.

35. Markowitz, 1991.

36. Falco, 1991.

Chapter 8: Staff

1. Ronnau, 1990, p. 27.

2. U.S. Department of Health and Human Services, 1981, p. 1.

Chapter 9: Where Do We Go From Here?

1. U.S. Advisory Board on Child Abuse and Neglect, 1993, p. 1.

2. Allen and Zalenski, 1993; Annie E. Casey Foundation, 1992; Annie E. Casey Foundation and Center for the Study of Social Policy, 1992; Barthel, 1992b; Children's Defense Fund, 1991, 1992; Kamerman and Kahn, 1989a; Moss, 1993; National Commission on Children, 1993a; Sallee and Mannes, 1991b, 1992; U.S. Advisory Board on Child Abuse and Neglect, 1991, 1993.

3. Annie E. Casey Foundation and Center for the Study of Social Policy, 1992.

4. Annie E. Casey Foundation, 1992, p. 14.

5. Children's Defense Fund, 1992, p. 69.

6. Kamerman and Kahn, 1989, p. xvii.

7. Allen and Zalenski, 1993, p. 3.

8. Children's Defense Fund, 1992, p. xix.

9. Gall, 1990, p. 3.

10. Allen and Zalenski, 1993, p. 2.

11. Barth, 1992, p. 43.

12. Richard P. Barth, "Theories Guiding Home-Based Intensive Family Preservation Services," in Whittaker et al., 1990, pp. 98–99.

13. Kaplan, 1986a, p. 57.

14. Kagan, 1991, p. 19.

15. Task Force on Successful Outcome in Family-Based Services, n.d., p. 2.

16. Nelson, 1993, p. 12.

17. Schuerman et al., 1991, pp. 13–14.

18. Feldman, 1987, p. 8.

19. Sallee and Mannes, 1991a, p. 19.

Bibliography

Aaronson, May. "The Case Manager-Home Visitor." *Child Welfare* 68, no. 3 (May–June 1989): 339–346.

Adams, Paul. "Marketing Social Change: The Case of Family Preservation." School of Social Work, University of Iowa, 1992.

Alexander, James F. "Defensive and Supportive Communications in Normal and Deviant Families." *Journal of Consulting and Clinical Psychology* 40, no. 2 (April 1973):223–231.

———. "Behavior Modification and Delinquent Youth." In *Behavior Modification in Rehabilitation Settings,* 158–177. Edited by John G. Cull and Richard E. Hardy. Springfield, Ill.: Charles C. Thomas, 1974.

Alexander, James F., and Bruce V. Parsons. "Short-Term Behavioral Intervention with Delinquent Families: Impact on Family Process and Recidivism." *Journal of Abnormal Psychology* 81, no. 3 (June 1973):219–225.

Allen, Marcia. "Helping Alcoholics Change." *Prevention Report* (Fall 1986a):1–2.

———. "Overcoming Barriers to Working with Alcoholic Families." *Prevention Report* (Summer 1986b):1–2.

———. "Why Are We Talking About Case Management Again?" *Prevention Report* (Spring 1990):1–2.

———. "Redefining Family Reunification." *Prevention Report* (Fall 1992):5–7.

Allen, Marcia, and John Zalenski. "Making a Difference for Families:

Family-Based Services in the 1990s." *Prevention Report* (Spring 1993):1–3.

Allen, Mary Lee, Patricia Brown, and Belva Finlay. *Helping Children by Strengthening Families: A Look at Family Support Programs.* Washington, D.C.: Children's Defense Fund, 1992.

Anderson, Gary R., ed. *Courage to Care: Responding to the Crisis of Children with AIDS.* Washington, D.C.: Child Welfare League of America, 1990.

Annie E. Casey Foundation. *1992 Annual Report.* Greenwich, Conn.: Annie E. Casey Foundation, 1992.

Annie E. Casey Foundation and Center for the Study of Social Policy. *Kids Count Data Book: State Profiles of Child Well-Being.* Washington, D.C.: Center for the Study of Social Policy, 1992.

Aponte, Harry J. "The Family-School Interview: An Eco-Structural Approach." *Family Process* 15, no. 3 (September 1976a):303–311.

———. "Underorganization in the Poor Family." In *Family Therapy: Theory and Practice,* 432–448. Edited by Philip J. Guerin, Jr. New York: Gardner Press, 1976b.

———. "Anatomy of a Therapist." In *Family Therapy Full Length Case Studies,* New York: Gardner Press, 1977. Edited by Peggy Papp. 101–116.

Aponte, Harry J., John J. Zarski, Catherine Bixenstine, and Pamela Cibik. "Home/Community-Based Services: A Two-Tier Approach." *American Journal of Orthopsychiatry* 61, no. 3 (July 1991):403–408.

Associate Control, Research and Analysis. *A Guide for Providing Social Services in Head Start.* Washington, D.C.: U.S. Department of Health and Human Services, February 1980.

AuClaire, Philip, and Ira M. Schwartz. "An Evaluation of the Effectiveness of Intensive Home-Based Services as an Alternative to Placement for Adolescents and their Families." Minneapolis: Hubert H. Humphrey Institute of Public Affairs, University of Minnesota, December 1986.

———. "Are Home Based Services Effective? A Public Child Welfare Agency's Experiment." *Children Today* 16, no. 3 (May–June 1987a):6–9.

———. "Home-Based Services as an Alternative to Placement for Adolescents and Their Families: A Follow-up Study of Placement Utilization." Minneapolis: Hubert H. Humphrey Institute of Public Affairs, University of Minnesota, June 1987b.

Auerswald, Edgar H. "Interdisciplinary versus Ecological Approach." *Family Process* 7, no. 2 (September 1968):202–215.

———. "Families, Change, and the Ecological Perspective." In *The Book of Family Therapy,* 684–705. Edited by Andrew Ferber, Marilyn Mendelsohn, and Augustus Napier. Boston: Houghton Mifflin, 1972.

Baldauf, Sue. "Parent Aides: A History of Success." *Common Ground* 10, no. 1 (February 1993):10.

Barnes, G., Chabon, R., and Hertzberg, L. "Team Treatment for Abusive Families." *Social Casework* 55 (1974):600–611.

Barnhill, Laurence R. "Healthy Family Systems." *Family Coordinator* 28, no. 1 (January 1979):94–100.

Barrett, Mary Jo, and Terry S. Trepper. "Unmasking the Incestuous Family." *Family Therapy Networker* 16, no. 3 (May–June 1992):39–46.

Barthel, Joan. "Family Preservation, Values and Beliefs." *Youth Policy* 14, no. 6 (October–November 1992a):32–36.

———. *For Children's Sake: The Promise of Family Preservation* New York: Annie E. Casey Foundation, Edna McConnell Clark Foundation, Foundation for Child Development, and Skillman Foundation, 1992b.

Bassuk, Ellen, Lenore Rubin, and Alison S. Lauriat. "Characteristics of Sheltered Homeless Families." *American Journal of Public Health* 76, no. 9 (September 1986):1097–1101.

Beck, Bertram M. *The Lower East Side Family Union: A Social Invention.* New York: Foundation for Child Development, March 1979.

Beck, D. F., and M. A. Jones. *Progress on Family Problems: A Nationwide Study of Clients' and Counselors' Views and Family Agency Services.* New York: Family Service Association of America, 1973.

Berg, Insoo Kim. *Family Based Services: A Solution-Focused Approach.* Milwaukee: Brief Family Therapy Center Press, 1992.

Berg, Insoo Kim, and Scott Miller. *Working with the Problem Drinker.* New York: W. W. Norton, 1992.

Berry, Marianne. "An Evaluation of Family Preservation Services: Fitting Agency Services to Family Needs." *Social Work* 37, no. 4 (July 1992):314–321.

Bertsche, Jon, and Frank Clark. "Improving the Utilization of Informal Helping Systems." *Sharing* 5, no. 2 (January–February 1981):2, 5.

Bieber, Robin. "Clinical Issues in the Treatment of Domestic Violence." *Common Ground* 10, no. 4 (November 1993):7.

Billingsley, Andrew. "Family Functioning in the Low-Income Black Community." *Social Casework* 50, no. 10 (December 1969):563–572.

———. *Climbing Jacob's Ladder.* New York: Simon and Schuster, 1992.

Birt, Charles J. "Family-Centered Project of St. Paul." *Social Work* 1, no. 4 (October 1956):41–47.

Bowlby, John. *Attachment.* 2nd ed. New York: Basic Books, 1983.

———. *A Secure Base: Parent-Child Attachment and Healthy Human Development.* New York: Basic Books, 1990.

Boyd-Franklin, Nancy. *Black Families in Therapy.* New York: Guilford Press, 1989.

Brisbane, Frances Larry, and Maxine Womble. *Working with African Amer-*

icans: The Professional's Handbook. Needham, Mass.: Ginn Press, 1992.

Bronfenbrenner, Urie. "Children and Families: 1984?" *Society* 18, no. 2 (January–February 1981):38–41.

Brooks, Gayle, and Diane DePanfilis. "Child Protection and Woman Abuse: Comparative Philosophies and Intervention Strategies." *Common Ground* 10, no. 4 (November 1993):1; 14.

Brown, Angela. *When Battered Women Kill.* New York: Free Press, 1987.

Brown, Carolyn L., and Susan Little. "Family Reunification." *Children Today* 19, no. 6 (November–December 1990):21–23, 33.

Brown, Gordon E., ed. *The Multi-Problem Dilemma: A Social Research Demonstration with Multi-Problem Families.* Metuchen, N.J.: Scarecrow Press, 1968.

Brown, June, and Marie Weil, eds. *Family Practice: A Curriculum Plan for Social Services.* Washington, D.C.: Child Welfare League of America, 1992.

Bryan, George, Jr. "Parent Aide Programs in the U.S." *Common Ground* 10, no. 1 (February 1993):10.

Bryce, Marvin E. *Placement Prevention and Family Reunification: Planning and Supervising the Home Based Family Centered Program.* Iowa City: National Clearinghouse for Home-Based Services to Children and Their Families, 1980.

———. *Family Support Programs for Troubled Juveniles.* Chicago: School of Social Service Administration, University of Chicago, September 1981.

Bryce, Marvin, and June C. Lloyd, eds. *Treating Families in the Home: An Alternative to Placement.* Springfield, Ill.: Charles C. Thomas, 1981.

Buell, Bradley, et al. *Community Planning for Human Services.* New York: Columbia University Press, 1952.

Burns, Virginia, and Sandra Venner. *Special Committee on Family Support and the Child Welfare System Report.* Boston, September 2, 1992.

Burt, Marvin, R. "The Comprehensive Emergency Services System: Expanding Services to Children and Families." *Children Today* 5, no. 2 (March–April 1976a):2–5.

———. "Final Results of the Nashville Comprehensive Emergency Services Project." *Child Welfare* 55, no. 9 (November 1976b):661–664.

Bush, Sherida. "A Family-Help Program That Really Works." *Psychology Today* 12 (May 1977):48, 50, 84, 88.

Cabral, R. J., and E. D. Callard. "A Home-Based Program to Serve High-Risk Families." *Journal of Home Economics* (Fall 1982):14–19.

Cade, Brian. "Therapy with Low Socio-Economic Families." *Social Work Today,* May 29, 1975, 142–145.

Carl, Douglas. *Counseling Same-Sex Couples.* New York: W. W. Norton, 1990.

Carter, Elizabeth A., and Monica McGoldrick, eds. *The Family Life Cycle: A Framework for Family Therapy.* New York: Gardner Press, 1980.

———. *The Changing Family Life Cycle: A Framework for Family Therapy.* 2d ed. Needham Heights, Mass.: Allyn and Bacon, 1989.

Carter, Judy Langford. "Building Family Capacity Attracts Diverse Partners." *Family Resource Coalition Report* 10, no. 1 (1991):5–7.

Cautley, Patricia W. *The Home and Community Treatment Process: Helping Families Change.* Madison, Wis.: Home and Community Treatment, Mendota Mental Health Institute, November 1979.

———. "Treating Dysfunctional Families at Home." *Social Work* 25, no. 5 (September 1980):380–386.

Cautley, Patricia W., and Mary Beth Plane. *Facilitating Family Change: A Look at Four Agencies Working Intensively with Families.* Madison, Wis.: Wisconsin Department of Health and Social Services, Division of Community Services, May 1983.

Center for the Study of Social Policy. "Indicators for Success in State Implementation of Family Preservation Services: A Guide for Strategic Planning." Working paper, the Family Preservation Technical Assistance Forum, November 1990.

———. *Kids Count Data Book.* Washington, D.C.: Center for the Study of Social Policy, 1992.

Chestang, Leon W. "Increasing the Effectiveness of Social Work Intervention with Minority Group Families." In *Toward Human Dignity: Social Work Practice, Fifth NASW Symposium,* 26–38. Edited by John W. Hanks. Washington, D.C.: National Association of Social Workers, 1978.

Child Welfare League of America. "Home Visiting: The Friendly Intervention." *Children's Voice* 2, no. 2 (Winter 1993a):8–9, 27.

———. "Rep. Robert T. Matsui." *Children's Voice* 2, no. 4 (Summer 1993b):4–5.

Children's Defense Fund. *The State of America's Children 1991.* Washington D.C.: Children's Defense Fund, 1991.

———. *The State of America's Children 1992.* Washington, D.C.: Children's Defense Fund, 1992.

Chilman, Catherine S. "Social Work Practice with Very Poor Families: Some Implications Suggested by the Available Research." *Welfare in Review* 4, no. 1 (January 1966):13–22.

Chun, Katherine, and Bart Aoki. "Ethnic Diversity and the Involvement of Parents in Preventing Adolescent Substance Abuse." *Family Resource Coalition Report* 10, no. 3 (1991):6.

Cimmarusti, Rocco A. "Family Preservation Practice Based upon a Multisystems Approach." *Child Welfare* 71, no. 3 (May–June 1992):241–256.

Clark, Ted, Tracey Zalis, and Frank Sacco. *Outreach Family Therapy*. New York: Jason Aronson, 1982.

Cole, Elizabeth, and Joy Duva. *Family Preservation: An Orientation for Administrators and Practitioners*. Washington, D.C.: Child Welfare League of America, 1990.

Collins, Raymond C. "Home Start and Its Implications for Family Policy." *Children Today* 9, no. 3 (May–June 1980):12–16.

Compher, John Victor. "Home Services to Families to Prevent Child Placement." *Social Work* 28, no. 5 (September–October 1983):360–364.

Compton, Beulah. "The Family Centered Project." Paper presented at the annual meeting of the Children's Aid Society of Winnipeg, April 25, 1962.

———. "A Participant Observer's Brief Summary of the Family-Centered Project." Minneapolis: School of Social Work, University of Minnesota, May 1979a.

———. "The Family Centered Project Revisited." Minneapolis: School of Social Work, University of Minnesota, May 1979b.

Cramer, Lina. "Work and Family Policy: An International Perspective." *Family Resource Coalition Report* 11, no. 2 (1992):16–17.

Crewdson, John. *By Silence Betrayed: Sexual Abuse of Children in America*. New York: Harper & Row, 1988.

Cross, Terry L., Barbara J. Bazron, Karl W. Dennis, and Mareasa R. Issacs. *Towards a Culturally Competent System of Care*. Vol. 1. Washington, D.C.: CASSP Technical Assistance Center, Georgetown University Child Development Center, March 1989.

Cummings, Nina, and Andrea Mooney. "Child Protective Workers and Battered Women's Advocates: A Strategy for Family Violence Intervention," *Response* 11, no. 2 (1988):4–9.

Curry-Rood, Leah, Larry A. Rood, and Sylvia E. Carter. *Head Start Parent Handbook*. Rev. ed. Mt. Rainer, Md.: Gryphon House, 1978.

Dahlheimer, Darryl, and Jennifer Feigal. "Bringing the Gap." *Family Therapy Networker* 15, no. 1 (January–February 1991):44–53.

DeMaria, Rita. "Family Therapy and Child Welfare: Therapy as Reparenting." *Family Therapy Networker* 10, no. 1 (January–February 1986):45–49.

Demmon-Berger, Debbie. "Saving Families Is Goal of FOCUS-HIP." *Sharing* 71, no. 1 (Winter 1987):2–4.

Department of Health and Rehabilitation Services. "Florida: Intensive Crisis

Counseling Programs." Tallahassee, Fl.: Department of Health and Rehabilitation Services, October 1, 1982.

de Shazer, Steve. "The Death of Resistance." *Family Process* 23 (1984):79–83.

———. *Keys to Solution in Brief Therapy*. New York: W. W. Norton, 1985.

———. *Clues: Investigating Solutions in Brief Therapy*. New York: W. W. Norton, 1988.

———. *Putting Difference to Work*. New York: W. W. Norton, 1991.

DeWitt, Kathryn Nash. "The Effectiveness of Family Therapy: A Review of Outcome Research." *Archives of General Psychiatry* 35, no. 5 (May 1978):549–561.

Dillon, Carolyn. "Working with Lesbian and Gay Clients." *Hawaii's Self-Help News* (October–November 1993):1–2, 6.

Dobash, R. Emerson, and Russell Dobash. *Violence Against Wives: A Case Against Patriarchy*. New York: Free Press, 1979.

Donnelly, Anne Cohn. "Healthy Families in America." *Children Today* 21, no. 2 (1992):25–28.

Drach, Kerry M. "Mental Health Program Intervention Through Networking." August 31, 1984.

Dunst, Carl J. "Family Support Principles: Checklists for Program Builders and Practitioners." *Family Systems Intervention Monograph* 2, no. 5 (May 1990).

———. "Evaluating Family Resource Programs." *Family Resource Coalition Report* 10, no. 1 (1991):15–16.

———. *Supporting and Strengthening Families: Aims, Principles, and Practices*. Morganton, N.C.: Center for Families Studies and Family, Infant and Preschool Program, Western Carolina Center, n.d.

Dunst, Carl, Carol Trivette, and Angela Deal. *Enabling and Empowering Families*. Cambridge, Mass.: Brookline Books, 1988.

Dunst, Carl J., Carol M. Trivette, and Rebekah B. Thompson. "Supporting and Strengthening Family Functioning: Toward a Congruence Between Principles and Practice." *Prevention in Human Services* 9, no. 1 (1990).

Dworkin, Andrea. *Woman Hating*. New York: Dutton, 1974.

Edelman, Peter B., and Beryl A. Radin. *Serving Children and Families Effectively: How the Past Can Help Chart the Future*. Washington, D.C.: Education and Human Services Consortium, 1991.

Edna McConnell Clark Foundation. *Keeping Families Together: Facts on Family Preservation Services*. New York: Edna McConnell Clark Foundation, 1992.

Elkin, Michael. *Families Under the Influence*. New York: W. W. Norton, 1984.

Epstein, Norman, and Anne Shainline. "Paraprofessional Parent-Aides and Disadvantaged Families." *Social Casework* 55, no. 4 (April 1974):230–236.

Falco, Kristine L. *Psychotherapy with Lesbian Clients.* New York: Brunner/ Mazel, 1991.

Faller, Kathleen Coulborn. "Permanency Planning with Scarce Resources: A Classification System for Child Welfare Cases." *Children Today* 13, no. 2 (March–April, 1984):2–5, 36.

"Family Union Keeps Families Together." *Practice Digest* 1, no. 1 (June 1979):22–23.

Fanshel, David. "Early Findings from a Study of Families at Risk Known to the Lower East Side Family Union." Paper presented at the 10th Anniversary Conference of the Lower East Side Family Union, New York City, May 16, 1985.

Faria, Geraldine. "Educating Students for Family-Based Practice with Lesbian Families." In *Empowering Families Papers from the Fifth Annual Conference on Family-Based Services,* 15–21. Riverdale, Ill.: National Association for Family-Based Services, 1992.

Farrow, Frank. "The View from States: Family Resource Programs and State Policy." *Family Resource Coalition Report* 10, no 1 (1991):12–13.

Feldman, Leonard. "Evaluating Family-Based Service Programs Within an Ecological Context." Paper presented at Empowering Families: A Celebration of Family Based Services Conference, Minneapolis, September 30, 1987.

———. "Evaluating the Impact of Family Preservation Services in New Jersey." Draft. Trenton, New Jersey: Bureau of Research, Evaluation and Quality Assurance, Division of Youth and Family Services, 1990.

Flaherty, Peggy. "Family Preservation and Family Support Act Is Now Law." *Common Ground* 10, no. 4 (November 1993):3.

Ford, Frederick R., and Joan Herrick. "Family Rules: Family Life Styles." *American Journal of Orthopsychiatry* 44, no. 1 (January 1974):61–69.

Foster, Pamela M., Frederick Phillips, Faye Z. Belgrave, Suzanne M. Randolph, and Noel Braithwaite. "An Africentric Model for AIDS Education, Prevention, and Psychological Services Within the African Community." *Journal of Black Psychology* 19, no. 2 (May 1993):123–141.

Fraser, Mark, and David Haapala. "Home-Based Family Treatment: A Quantitative-Qualitative Assessment." *Journal of Applied Social Sciences* 12 (Fall–Winter 1987–1988):1–23.

Fraser, Mark, Peter J. Pecora, and David A. Haapala. "Families in Crisis: Findings from the Family-Based Intensive Treatment Project." Federal Way, Wash.: Behavioral Sciences Institute; Salt Lake City: Social Research Institute, University of Utah, 1988.

————. "Intensive Family Preservation Services: An Update from the Family-Based Intensive Treatment Research Project." In *Prevention Report*. Oakdale, Iowa: National Resource Center on Family-Based Services, University of Iowa School of Social Work, 1990.

Freud, Elissa. "Family Support Programs for Families Who Have Children with Severe Emotional, Behavioral or Mental Disabilities: The State of the Art." Cambridge, Mass.: Human Services Research Institute, 1989.

Friedman, Robert M., and Sue Street. *Family-Focused Interventions: An Annotated Bibliography*. Tampa, Fla.: Research and Training Center for Improved Services for Seriously Emotionally Disturbed Children, October 1985.

Friedman, Roger S. "Homebuilders, Family Systems, and False Dichotomies: Reflections on Cross-Currents in Family Preservation Thinking and Steps Toward Integration." *Prevention Report* (Spring 1993):7–9.

Friedman, Steven, and Margot Taylor Fanger. *Expanding Therapeutic Possibilities: Getting Results in Brief Psychotherapy*. Lexington, Mass.: Lexington Books, 1991.

Froland, Charles, Diane L. Pancoast, Nancy J. Chapman, and Priscilla J. Kimboko. *Helping Networks and Human Services*. Sage Library of Social Research, 128. Beverly Hills, Calif.: Sage, 1981.

Gall, Mary Sheila. "Putting Families First." *Children Today* 19, no. 6 (November–December 1990):2–3.

Gatti, Frank, and Cathy Colman. "Community Network Therapy: An Approach to Aiding Families with Troubled Children." *American Journal of Orthopsychiatry* 46, no. 4 (October 1976):608–617.

Geismar, Ludwig L. *Family and Community Functioning: A Manual of Measurement for Social Work Practice and Policy*. Metuchen, N.J.: Scarecrow Press, 1971a.

Geismar, Ludwig G. "Implications of a Family Life Improvement Project." *Social Casework* 52, no. 7 (July 1971b):455–465.

Geismar, Ludwig L., and Jane Krisberg. *The Forgotten Neighborhood: Site of an Early Skirmish in the War on Poverty*. Metuchen, N.J.: Scarecrow Press, 1967.

Geismar, L. L., and Michael A. LaSorte. *Understanding the Multi-Problem Family: A Conceptual Analysis and Exploration in Early Identification*. New York: Association Press, 1964.

Geismar, Ludwig G., and Katherine M. Wood. *Family and Delinquency: Resocializing the Young Offender*. New York: Human Sciences Press, 1986.

Gelinas, Denise J. "The Persisting Negative Effects of Incest." *Psychiatry* 46 (November, 1983):312–321.

Gelles, Richard J. "Gelles: Child Protection Needs to Replace Family Reunification As Goal of Child Welfare Agencies." *Brown University Family Therapy Letter* 4, no. 6 (June 1992):1–2.

George, Rickey. *Counseling the Chemically Dependent.* Boston: Allyn and Bacon, 1990.

Germain, Carel B., ed. *Social Work Practice: People and Environments: An Ecological Perspective.* New York: Columbia University Press, 1979.

Giblin, P. T., and E. D. Callard. "Issues in Evaluation of Action Research: A Social Service Model." *Social Work Research and Abstracts* 16, no. 4 (Winter 1980):3–12.

Gilbert, Richard, Andrew Christensen, and Gayla Margolin. "Patterns of Alliances in Nondistressed and Multiproblem Families." *Family Process* 23, no. 1 (March 1984):75–87.

Giles-Sims, J. *Wife Battering: A Systems Theory Approach.* New York: Guilford Press, 1983.

Glasser, William. *Reality Therapy: A New Approach to Psychiatry.* New York: Harper & Row, 1965.

Glick, Ira D., and Jay Haley. *Family Therapy and Research: An Annotated Bibliography of Articles and Books Published 1950–1970.* New York: Grune and Stratton, 1971.

Goldson, Mary Funnyé. *Helping Multiproblem Families to Help Themselves: The Practice Model of the Lower East Side Family Union.* New York: Lower East Side Family Union, August 1989.

Godstein, Harriet. "Providing Services to Children in Their Own Homes: An Approach That Can Reduce Foster Placement." *Children Today* 2, no. 4 (July–August 1973):2–7.

Goldstein, J., A. Freud, and A. Solnit. *Beyond the Best Interests of the Child.* New York: Free Press, 1973.

———. *Before the Best Interests of the Child.* New York: Free Press, 1979.

Goldstein, Steven. "Bye Bye Brady Bunch: A Poor Family Discovers Its Competence." *Family Therapy Networker* 10, no. 1 (January–February 1986):31–32, 76–78.

Gondolf, Edward W. *Men Who Batter: An Integrated Approach to Stopping Wife Abuse.* Holmes Beach, Fla.: Learning Publications, 1985.

Gondolf, Edward W., with Ellen Fisher. *Battered Women as Survivors: An Alternative to Treating Learned Helplessness.* Lexington, Mass.: Lexington Books, 1988.

Gordon, L. *Heroes of Their Own Lives: The Politics and History of Family Violence.* New York: Viking Press, 1988.

Gray, Sylvia Sims, Ann Hartman, and Ellen S. Saalberg, eds. *Empowering the Black Family: A Roundtable Discussion with Ann Hartman, James Leigh, Jacquelynn Moffett, Elaine Pinderhughes, Barbara Solomon, and Carol Stack.* Ann Arbor, Mich.: National Child Welfare Training Center, University of Michigan, School of Social Work, 1985.

Gray, Sylvia Sims, and Lynn M. Nybell. "Issues in African-American Family

Preservation." *Child Welfare* 69, no. 6 (November–December 1990):513–523.

Groth, Nicholas. "The Incest Offender." In Suzanne M. Sgroi, ed. *Handbook of Clinical Intervention in Child Sexual Abuse*, 215–218. Lexington, Mass.: Lexington Books, 1982.

Haapala, David, Vera O. Pina, and Cecelia Sudia. *Empowering Families: Papers from the Fourth Annual Conference on Family-Based Services*. Riverdale, Ill.: National Association for Family-Based Services, 1991.

Haley, Jay. *Problem-Solving Therapy*. San Francisco: Jossey-Bass, 1976.

———. *Leaving Home*. New York: McGraw-Hill, 1980.

Halper, Gertrude, and Mary Ann Jones. *Serving Families at Risk of Dissolution: Public Preventive Services in New York City*. New York: City of New York Human Resources Administration, February 1981.

Halpern, Robert. "Lack of Effects for Home-Based Early Intervention? Some Possible Explanations." *American Journal of Orthopsychiatry* 54, no. 1 (January 1984):33–42.

———. "Home-Based Early Intervention: Dimensions of Current Practice." *Child Welfare* 65, no. 4 (July–August 1986):387–398.

———. "Supportive Services for Families in Poverty: Dilemmas of Reform." *Social Service Review* 65, no. 3 (September 1991).

Hancock, B. and Pelton, L. "Home Visits: History and Functions." *Social Casework* 70 (1989):21–27.

Hanson, Janice L., Elizabeth S. Jeppson, and Beverley H. Johnson. "Promoting Family-Centered Services in Health Care and Beyond." *Family Resource Coalition Report* 11, no. 3 (Winter 1992–93):12–14.

Harrison, Algea O. "The Importance of Including Grandparents in Services for African American Families." *Family Resource Coalition Report* 12, no. 1 (Spring 1993):24–25.

Hartman, Ann. "The Family: A Central Focus for Practice." *Social Work* 26, no. 1 (January 1981):7–13.

———. "Family Preservation Under Attack." *Social Work* 38, no. 5 (September 1993):509–512.

Hartman, Ann, and Joan Laird. *Family-Centered Social Work Practice*. New York: Free Press, 1983.

Harvey, Cathie, and Marilee Comfort with Nancy Johns. "Integrating Parent Support into Residential Treatment Programs." *Family Resource Coalition Report* 10, no. 3 (1991):4–5.

Henggeler, Scott W. "A Multisystemic Approach with Juvenile Offenders: A Cost-Saving Strategy for Reducing Recidivism and Institutionalization." *Prevention Report* (Spring 1993):9–11.

Herman, Judith Lewis. *Trauma and Recovery*. New York: Basic Books, 1992.

Hess, Peg M., and Kathleen O' Proch. *Family Visiting of Children in Out-of-Home Care: A Practical Guide*. Washington, D.C.: Child Welfare League of America, 1989.

Hess, Peg McCartt, Gail Folaron, and Ann Buschmann Jefferson. "Effectiveness of Family Reunification Services: An Innovative Evaluative Model." *Social Work* 37, no. 4 (July 1992):304–311.

Heying, Kenneth R. "Family-Based, In-Home Services for the Severely Emotionally Disturbed Child." *Child Welfare* 64, no. 5 (September–October 1985):519–527.

Hilberman, Elaine. "Overview: The "Wife-Beater's Wife" Reconsidered." *American Journal of Psychiatry* 137, no. 11 (November 1980):1336–1346.

Hill, Robert B. *The Strengths of Black Families*. New York: Emerson Hall, 1972.

———. "Dispelling Myths and Building on Strengths: Supporting African American Families." *Family Resource Coalition Report* 12, no. 1 (Spring 1993):3–5.

Hinckley, Edward C. "Homebuilders: The Maine Experience." *Children Today* 13, no. 5 (September–October 1984):14–17, 36.

———. "How to Develop Coordinated, Interdepartmental Public-Agency Support for Home-Based Services: The Maine Experience." *Permanency Report* 3, no. 1 (Winter 1985):2.

Hinckley, Edward C., and W. Frank Ellis. "An Effective Alternative to Residential Placement: Home-based Services." *Journal of Clinical Child Psychology* 14, no. 3 (Fall, 1985):209–213.

Hobbs, Nicholas, Paul R. Dokecki, Kathleen V. Hoover-Dempsey, Robert M. Moroney, May W. Shayne, and Karen H. Weeks. *Strengthening Families*. San Francisco: Jossey-Bass, 1984.

Hodges, Vanessa G., and Betty Blythe. "Improving Service Delivery to High-Risk Families: Home-based Practice." *Families in Society: The Journal of Contemporary Human Services* 73 (May 1992):259–265.

Hoffman, Lynn, and Lorence Long. "A Systems Dilemma." *Family Process* 8, no. 2 (September 1969):211–234.

Holbrook, T. L. "Going Among Them: The Evolution of the Home Visit." *Journal of Sociology and Social Welfare* 10, no. 1 (1983):112–135.

Hollis, F., and M. E. Wood. *Casework: A Psychosocial Therapy*. New York: Random House, 1981.

Horn, Jack C. "House-calls for Families in Crisis." *Psychology Today* 10, no. 7 (December 1976):113–114.

Howard, Bill. "The (Over?)Selling of Homebuilders." *Youth Today* 1, no. 1 (September–October 1992):9–10.

Howing, Phyllis T., and John S. Wodarski. "Legal Requisites for Social Workers in Child Abuse and Neglect Situations." *Social Work* 37, no. 4 (July 1992):330–336.

Hutchinson, Janet. *Family-Centered Social Services: A Model for Child Welfare Agencies*. Oakdale, Iowa: National Resource Center on Family Based Services, University of Iowa, July 28, 1983.

Hutchinson, Janet R., and Kristine E. Nelson. "How Public Agencies Can Provide Family-Centered Services." *Social Casework* 66, no. 6 (June 1985):367–371.

Hutchinson, Elizabeth D. "Mandatory Reporting Laws: Child Protective Case Finding Gone Awry?" *Social Work* 38, no. 1 (January, 1993):56–63.

Issacs, Mareasa R., and Marva P. Benjamin. *Towards a Culturally Competent System of Care*. Vol. 2. Washington, D.C.: CASSP Technical Assistance Center, Georgetown University Child Development Center, December, 1991.

Jacobi, John E. *Meeting the Needs of Children and Youth in Massachusetts Communities: The Local Area Study and Demonstration Project*. Boston: Massachusetts Committee on Children and Youth, 1968.

Janchill, Sister Mary Paul. *Guidelines to Decision-Making in Child Welfare*. New York: Human Service Workshops, 1981.

Janzen, Curtis, and Oliver Harris. *Family Treatment in Social Work Practice*. Itasca, Ill.: F. E. Peacock, 1980.

Joint Commission on Mental Illness and Health. *Actions for Mental Health*. New York: Basic Books, 1961.

Jones, Ann. *Women Who Kill*. New York: Holt, Rinehart & Winston, 1980.

Jones, Ann, and Susan Schechter. *When Love Goes Wrong*. New York: HarperCollins, 1992.

Jones, Mary Ann. "Reducing Foster Care Through Services to Families." *Children Today* 5, no. 6 (November–December 1976):6–10.

———. *A Second Chance for Families—Five Years Later: Follow-up of a Program to Prevent Foster Care Executive Summary*. New York: Child Welfare League of America, November 1983.

Jones, Mary Ann, Stephen Magura, and Ann W. Shyne. "Effective Practice with Families in Protective and Preventive Services: What Works?" *Child Welfare* 60, no. 2 (February 1981):67–80.

Jones, Mary Ann, Renee Neuman, and Ann W. Shyne. *A Second Chance for Families: Evaluation of a Program to Reduce Foster Care*. New York: Child Welfare League of America, 1976.

Kagan, Daniel. "Saving Families Fosters Hope for America's Troubled Youth." *Insight*, April 29, 1991, 16–19.

Kagan, Richard, and Shirley Schlosberg. *Families in Perpetual Crisis.* New York:
W. W. Norton, 1989.

Kagan, Sharon L. "America's Family Support Movement." *Family Resource Coalition Report* 10, no. 1 (1991):17–19.

Kagan, Sharon L., Douglas R. Powell, Bernice Weissbourd, and Edward F. Zigler, eds. *America's Family Support Programs Perspectives and Prospects.* New Haven: Yale University Press, 1987.

Kahn, Alfred J., and Sheila B. Kamerman. *Not for the Poor Alone.* Philadelphia: Temple University Press, 1975.

Kamerman, Sheila, and Alfred J. Kahn. *Social Services in the United States: Policies and Programs.* Philadelphia: Temple University Press, 1976.

———. *Social Services for Children, Youth and Families in the U.S.* Greenwich, Conn.: Annie E. Casey Foundation, June 1989a.

———. "The Possibilities for Child and Family Policy: A Cross-National Perspective." In *Caring for America's Children,* 84–98. Edited by Frank J. Macchiarola and Alan Gortner. New York: Academy of Political Science, 1989b.

Kaplan, Lauren Weller. "The 'Multi-Problem' Family Phenomenon: An Interactional Perspective." Ph.D. dissertation, University of Massachusetts, 1984.

Kaplan, Lisa. *Working with Multiproblem Families.* Lexington, Mass.: Lexington Books, 1986a.

———. "Philosophy and Practice That Meet the Needs of Multiproblem Families." *Permanency Report* 4, no. 3 (Summer 1986b):2.

———. "Working with Multiproblem Families." *Justice for Children* 1, no. 4 (Spring 1986c):20–21.

———. "Family Preservation Services: The State of the Art." *Common Ground* 3, no. 2 (August 1987):4–5.

Kinch, Richard, ed. *Strengthening Families Through Informal Support Systems.* Racine, Wis.: Johnson Foundation, April 1979.

King, Charles H., and Clara Rabinowitz. "The Impact of Public Welfare Practice on Family Attitudes with Special Reference to Delinquent Children." *American Journal of Orthopsychiatry* 35 (April 1965):609–613.

Kinney, Jill. "Homebuilders: An In-Home Crisis Intervention Program." *Children Today* 7, no. 1 (January–February 1978):15–17, 35.

———. "Brief Home-Based Intervention Is Effective." *Permanency Report* 2, no. 2 (Spring 1984):2.

Kinney, Jill, Dittmar Kelly, and Wendy Firth. "Keeping Families Together: The Homebuilders Model." *Children Today* 19, no. 6 (November–December 1990):14–19.

Kinney, Jill McCleave, Barbara Madsen, Thomas Fleming, and David Haapala. "Homebuilders: Keeping Families Together." *Journal of Consulting and Clinical Psychology* 45, no. 4 (August 1977):667–673.

Klein, Nanci C., James F. Alexander, and Bruce V. Parsons. "Impact of Family Systems Intervention on Recidivism and Sibling Delinquency: A Model for Primary Prevention and Program Evaluation." *Journal of Consulting and Clinical Psychology* 45, no. 3 (June 1977):469–474.

Knitzer, Jane. *Unclaimed Children: The Failure of Public Responsibility to Children and Adolescents in Need of Mental Health Services.* Washington, D.C.: Children's Defense Fund, 1982.

———. *Collaborations Between Child Welfare and Mental Health: Emerging Patterns and Challenges.* New York: Bank Street College of Education, May 1989.

Knitzer, Jane, Mary Lee Allen, and Brenda McGowan. *Children Without Homes: An Examination of Public Responsibility to Children in Out-of-Home Care.* Washington, D.C.: Children's Defense Fund, 1978.

Knitzer, Jane, and Elizabeth S. Cole. *Family Preservation Services: The Policy Challenge to State Child Welfare and Child Mental Health Systems.* New York: Bank Street College of Education, May 1989a.

———. *Family Preservation Services: The Program Challenge for Child Welfare and Child Mental Health Agencies.* New York: Bank Street College of Education, May 1989b.

Kozol, Jonathan. *Rachel and Her Children: Homeless Families in America.* New York: Fawcett Columbine, 1988.

Kübler-Ross, Elisabeth. *Death: The Final Stage of Growth.* Englewood Cliffs, N.J.: Prentice-Hall, 1975.

Kus, Robert J. *Keys to Caring: Assisting Your Gay and Lesbian Clients.* Boston: Alyson Publications, 1990.

Lanning, Kenneth V. *Child Molesters: A Behavioral Analysis for Law Enforcement Officers Investigating Cases of Child Sexual Exploitation.* Arlington, Va.: National Center for Missing and Exploited Children, December 1992.

Laster, Berger Laura. "Gay and Lesbian Parenting in the '90s." *Boston Parent's Paper* (September 1992):8–11.

Lawder, Elizabeth A., John E. Poulin, and Roberta G. Andrews. *Helping the Multi-Problem Family: A Study of Services to Children in Their Own Homes.* Philadelphia: Children's Aid Society of Pennsylvania, 1984.

Letich, Larry. "Profiles of the Perpetrators." *Family Therapy Networker* 16, no. 3 (May–June 1992):46–47.

———. "A Clinician's Researcher." *Family Therapy Networker* 17, no. 5 (September–October 1993):77–82.

Levine, M., and A. Levine. *Helping Children: A Social History.* New York: Oxford University Press, 1992.

Levy, Alan J., and John S. Brekke. "Spouse Battering and Chemical Dependency: Dynamics, Treatment, and Service Delivery." *Journal of Chemi-*

cal Dependency Treatment Special Issue: Aggression, Family Violence, and Chemical Dependency, 3, no. 1 (1989):81–97.

Lewis, Jerry M., W. Robert Beavers, John T. Gossett, and Virginia Austin Phillips. No Single Thread: Psychological Health in Family Systems. New York: Brunner/Mazel, 1976.

Littell, Julia H. Building Strong Foundations: Evaluation Strategies for Family Resource Programs. Chicago: Family Resource Coalition, 1986.

Littner, N. Some Traumatic Effects of Separation and Placement. New York: Child Welfare League of America, 1967.

Lloyd, June C., and Martin E. Bryce. Placement Prevention and Family Reunification: A Handbook for the Family-Centered Service Practitioner. Iowa City: National Resource Center on Family Based Services, University of Iowa, 1984.

Locke, Don C. Increasing Multicultural Understanding: A Comprehensive Model. Newbury Park, Calif.: Sage Publications, 1992.

McAdoo, Harriette. "Family Therapy in the Black Community." American Journal of Orthopsychiatry 47, no. 1 (January 1977):75–79.

———, editor. Black Families. 2d ed. Newbury Park, Calif.: Sage Publications, 1988.

McAdoo, John L. "Understanding Fathers: Human Services Perspectives in Theory and Practice." Family Resource Coalition Report 12, no. 1 (Spring 1993):18–20.

McCarthy, Loretta M. "Mother-Child Incest: Characteristics of Offender." Child Welfare 65, no. 5 (September–October 1986):447–458.

McCroskey, Jacquelyn, and Judith Nelson. "Practice-Based Research in a Family-Support Program: The Family Connection Project Example." Child Welfare 68, no. 6 (November–December 1989):573–587.

McGoldrick, Monica, John K. Pearce, and Joseph Giordano, eds. Ethnicity and Family Therapy. New York: Guilford Press, 1982.

McGowan, Brenda G., and William Meezan. Child Welfare: Current Dilemmas, Future Directions. Itasca, Ill.: F. E. Peacock, 1983.

McKinney, Geraldine E. "Adapting Family Therapy to Multideficit Families." Social Casework 51, no. 6 (June 1970):327–333.

Madanes, Cloé. Strategic Family Therapy. San Francisco: Jossey-Bass, 1981.

———. Sex, Love, and Violence: Strategies for Transformation. New York: W. W. Norton, 1990.

Magura, Stephen. "Are Services to Prevent Foster Care Effective?" Children and Youth Services Review, no. 3 (1981):193–212.

Mann, James. Time-Limited Psychotherapy. Cambridge, Mass.: Harvard University Press, 1973.

Mannino, Fortune V., and Milton F. Shore. "Ecologically Oriented Family Intervention." Family Process 11, no. 4 (December 1972):499–505.

Markowitz, Laura M. "Homosexuality: Are We Still in the Dark?" *Family Therapy Networker* 15, no. 1 (January–February 1991):27–35.

———. "Making House Calls." *Family Therapy Networker* 16, no. 4 (July–August 1992a):27–37.

———. "Reclaiming the Light." *Family Therapy Networker* 16, no. 3 (May–June 1992b):17–24.

Martin, April. *The Lesbian and Gay Parenting Handbook: Creating and Raising Our Families.* New York: HarperCollins, 1993.

Martin, Del. *Battered Wives.* San Francisco: Volcano Press, 1981.

Maslow, Abraham. *Motivation and Personality.* New York: Harper & Row, 1954.

Massachusetts Department of Social Services. *A Family-Centered Approach to Case Management Practice.* Boston: Massachusetts Department of Social Services, February 1993.

Maybanks, Sheila, and Marvin Bryce, eds. *Home-Based Services for Children and Families: Policy, Practice, and Research.* Springfield, Ill.: Charles C. Thomas, 1979.

Mederos, Fernando R. "Creating a New Taboo—Reframing Work with Violent Men." *Common Ground* 10, no. 4 (November 1993):1, 8.

Melaville, Atelia I. *What It Takes: Structuring Interagency Partnerships to Connect Children and Families with Comprehensive Services.* Washington, D.C.: Education and Human Services Consortium, 1991.

Meyer, Carol H. "Individualizing the Multiproblem Family." *Social Casework* 44, no. 5 (May 1963):267–272.

Meyerstein, Israela. "Family Therapy Training for Paraprofessionals in a Community Mental Health Center." *Family Process* 16, no. 4 (December 1977):477–493.

Mihaly, Lisa Klee. "Domestic Violence Is a Children's Issue." *Common Ground* 10, no. 4 (November 1993):11.

Minuchin, Patricia. "A Systems Approach to Foster Care." *Prevention Report* (Fall 1992):1–3.

Minuchin, Salvador. "The Plight of the Poverty-Stricken Family in the United States." *Child Welfare* 49, no. 3 (March 1970a):124–130.

———. "The Use of an Ecological Framework in the Treatment of a Child." In *The Child in His Family,* 41–57. Edited by E. James Anthony and Cyrille Koupernik. New York: Wiley-Interscience, 1970b.

———. *Families and Family Therapy.* Cambridge, Mass.: Harvard University Press, 1974.

Minuchin, Salvador, and Braulio Montalvo. "Techniques for Working with Disorganized Low Socioeconomic Families." *American Journal of Orthopsychiatry* 37, no. 5 (October 1967):880–887.

Minuchin, Salvador, Braulio Montalvo, Bernard G. Guerney, Jr., Bernice L. Rosman, and Florence Schumer. *Families of the Slums: An Exploration of Their Structure and Treatment.* New York: Basic Books, 1967.

Mirkin, Marsha Pravder, and Stuart L. Koman, eds. *Handbook of Adolescents and Family Therapy.* New York: Gardner Press, 1985.

Mitchell, Brian J. *Helping Families in Great Need: An American Perspective.* Footscray, Australia: St. Anthony's Family Service, April 1987.

Mitchell, C., P. Tovar, and Jane Knitzer. "The Bronx Homebuilders Program: An Evaluation of the First 45 Families." New York: Bank Street College of Education, 1989.

Morse, Abraham E., James N. Hyde, Jr., Eli H. Newberger, and Robert B. Reed. "Environmental Correlates of Pediatric Social Illness: Preventive Implications of an Advocacy Approach." *American Journal of Public Health* 67, no. 7 (July 1977):612–615.

Morton, E. Susan, and R. Kevin Grigsby, eds. *Advancing Family Preservation Practice.* Newbury Park, Calif.: Sage, 1993.

Moss, Myla. "Child Abuse and Neglect: A Devastating Crisis We Cannot Ignore." *Caring-National Association of Homes and Services for Children* 9, no. 3 (Summer 1993):18–20.

Mostwin, Danuta. *Social Dimension of Family Treatment.* Washington, D.C.: National Association of Social Workers, 1980.

Mowrer, Charles. "The Family Worker and the Incestuous Family: Integrating Levels of Understanding—Part 1: Issues and Models." *Prevention Report* (Winter 1986–87):1–2.

———. "The Family Worker and the Incestuous Family: Integrating Levels of Understanding—Part 2: Implications for Risk Assessment and Treatment." *Prevention Report* (Spring 1987):1–3.

Moynihan, Daniel Patrick. *Family and Nation.* New York: Harcourt Brace Jovanovich, 1986.

Mulroy, Elizabeth. "Single-Parent Families and the Housing Crisis: Implications for Macropractice." *Social Work* 35, no. 6 (November 1990):542–546.

Murphy, Patrick. "Family Preservation and Its Victims." *New York Times,* June 19, 1993, 21.

Murray, H. A. *Explorations in Personality.* New York: Oxford University Press, 1938.

Napier, Augustus Y., and Carl A. Whitaker. *The Family Crucible.* New York: Bantam Books, 1978.

National Association of Social Workers, "Foster Care Up Despite 'Permanency' Efforts." *NASW News* 38, no. 7 (July 1993):9.

National Center on Child Abuse and Neglect. *1990 Summary Data Component.* Working Paper 1. April 1992.

National Coalition Against Domestic Violence. Brochure.

National Commission on Children. *Beyond Rhetoric: A New American*

Agenda for Children and Families. Washington, D.C.: National Commission on Children, 1991.

———. *Protecting Vulnerable Children and Their Families.* Washington, D.C.: National Commission on Children, 1993a.

———. *Strengthening and Supporting Families.* Washington, D.C.: National Commission on Children, 1993b.

———. *Making Programs and Policies Work.* Washington, D.C.: National Commission on Children, 1993c.

National Institute on Drug Abuse. *Drug Abuse and Drug Abuse Research.* Rockville, Md.: U.S. Government Printing Office, 1987.

The National Resource Center on Family Based Services. *Annotated Bibliography on Family Based Services.* Oakdale, Iowa: National Resource Center on Family Based Services, University of Iowa, 1982.

———. *Resources for Family Based Service Practice: An Annotated Sourcebook.* Iowa City: National Resource Center on Family Based Services, July 1986a.

———. *Annotated Directory of Selected Family-Based Service Programs.* Iowa City: National Resource Center on Family Based Services, University of Iowa, July 1986b.

———. *An Analysis of Factors Contributing to Failure in Family-Based Child Welfare Services in Eleven Family-Based Services Agencies: Executive Summary.* Iowa City: National Resource Center on Family Based Services, University of Iowa, April 1988.

Nelson, Kristine. "How Do We Know That Family-Based Services Are Effective?" *Prevention Report* (Fall 1990):1–3.

———. "Assessing Risk of Placement in Family Preservation Services." *Prevention Report* (Spring 1993):12–15.

Nelson, Kristine E., and Marcia Allen. "Public-Private Provision of Family-Based Services: Research Findings." Unpublished paper. Iowa City: National Resource Center on Family Based Services, 1989.

Nelson, Kristine E., and Miriam J. Landsman. *Alternative Models of Family Preservation: Family-Based Services in Context.* Springfield, Ill.: Charles C. Thomas, 1993.

Nelson, Kristine E., Miriam L. Landsman, and Wendy Deutelbaum. "Three Models of Family-Centered Placement Prevention Services." *Child Welfare* 69, no. 1 (January–February 1990):3–21.

Nelson, Kristine, Miriam Landsman, and Margaret Tyler. "Intensive Family Services: Research Project: Preliminary Report." Iowa City: National Resource Center on Family Based Services, University of Iowa, October 1991.

Norman, Abigail. *Keeping Families Together: The Case for Family Preservation.* New York: Edna McConnell Clark Foundation, 1985.

Norton, Dolores. "A Conversation with FRC President Bernice Weissbourd." *Family Resource Coalition Report* 10, no. 1 (1991):10–11.

Ogren, Evelyn H., and Brian J. Mitchell. "Evaluation of Family Support Services: From the Standpoint of the Service Provider." Paper presented at the Fifth National Evaluation Conference, Melbourne, Australia, July 27–29, 1988.

O'Hanlon, William Hudson, and Michele Weiner-Davis. *In Search of Solutions: A New Direction in Psychotherapy.* New York: W. W. Norton, 1989.

Ooms, Theodora. *Coordination, Collaboration, Integration: Strategies for Serving Families More Effectively.* Washington, D.C.: Family Impact Seminar, AAMFT Research and Education Foundation, 1990.

Orcott, Ben A. "Family Treatment of Poverty Level Families." *Social Casework* 58, no. 2 (February 1977):92–100.

Overton, Alice, et al. *Casework Notebook.* St. Paul, Minn.: United Way of the St. Paul Area, 1978.

Overton-Adkins, Betty J. "In Our Mothers' Homes There Is Still God: African American Spirituality." *Family Resource Coalition Report,* 12, no. 1 (Spring 1993):26–27.

Parsons, Bruce V., and James F. Alexander. "Short-Term Family Intervention: A Therapy Outcome Study." *Journal of Consulting and Clinical Psychology* 41, no. 2 (October 1973):195–201.

Partnership for the Homeless. *Moving Forward: A National Agenda to Address Homelessness in 1990 and Beyond and A Status Report on Homelessness in America: A 46-City Survey, 1988–89.* New York: Partnership for the Homeless, 1989.

Partridge, Susan E. *Personal and Professional Challenges in Working with Multiproblem Families.* Portland, Me.: Human Services Development Institute, January 1988.

Patterson, Ken. "Investing in an Agency's 'Work Family' ": Idaho's Experience in Implementing a Family-Centered Practice Model." *Prevention Report* (Spring 1992):6–7.

Pavenstedt, E., ed. *The Drifters: Children of Disorganized Lower Class Families.* Boston: Little, Brown, 1967.

Payne, Carol, editor. *Programs to Strengthen Families: A Resource Guide.* Chicago: Family Resource Coalition and Yale University, 1983.

Pearl, Arthur, and Frank Riessman. *New Careers for the Poor: The Nonprofessional in Human Service.* New York: The Free Press, 1965.

Pecora, Peter J., Mark W. Fraser, David Haapala, and Jeffrey A. Bartlomé. "Defining Family Preservation Services: Three Intensive Home-Based Treatment Programs." Salt Lake City: Social Research Institute, University of Utah, September 4, 1987.

Pecora, Peter J., et al. "The Family-Based Intensive Treatment Project: Selected Research Findings from the First Year of Data Collection." Salt

Lake City: Social Research Institute, and Federal Way; Washington, D.C.: Behavioral Sciences Institute, September 8, 1986.

Pelton, Leroy H. "Resolving the Crisis in Child Welfare: Simply Expanding the Present System Is Not Enough." *Public Welfare* 48, no. 4 (Fall 1990):19–25, 45.

———. "Beyond Permanency Planning: Restructuring the Public Child Welfare System." *Social Work* 36, no. 4 (July 1991):337–343.

———. "A Functional Approach to Reorganizing Family and Child Welfare Interventions." *Children and Youth Services Review* 14 (1992):289–303.

———. "Enabling Public Child Welfare Agencies to Promote Family Preservation." *Social Work* 38, no. 4 (July 1993):491–493.

Phillips, Frederick B. "NTU Psychotherapy: An Afrocentric Approach." *Journal of Black Psychology* 17, no. 1 (Fall 1990):55–74.

Pies, Cheri. *Considering Parenthood.* Minneapolis: Spinsters Book Company, 1988.

Pine, Barbara A., Robin Warsh, and Anthony N. Maluccio, eds. *Together Again: Family Reunification in Foster Care.* Washington, D.C.: Child Welfare League of America, 1993.

Pittman, Frank S. "The Family That Hides Together." In *Family Therapy Full Length Case Studies,* 1–21. Edited by Peggy Papp. New York: Gardner Press, 1977.

Polansky, Norman, Rebecca J. Cabral, Stephen Magura, and Michael H. Phillips. "Comparative Norms for the Childhood Level of Living Scale." *Journal of Social Service Research* 6, no. 3/4 (Spring–Summer 1983):45–55.

Porter, Toni. "Partners for Success: Family Support for Formerly Homeless Families." *Family Resource Coalition Report* 11, no. 3 (Winter 1992–1993):6–7.

Powell, Douglas R. "Staff Development in Family Resource Programs." *Family Resource Coalition Report* 10, no. 1 (1991):14–15.

Powell, Wayne. "Strengthening Parents' Social Networks: An Ecological Approach to Primary Prevention." Paper presented at the American Psychological Association, Montreal, September 1980.

Prochaska, Janice, M., and Ronald E. Arsenault. "Intra-Agency Contracting: High-Quality, Comprehensive Service Delivery at Lowered Cost." *Child Welfare* 63, no. 6 (November–December 1984):533–539.

Purdie, Gail, and Theodore Levine. "Family Based Care: A Ten Year Review of Service Delivery and Outcomes and Its Impact on the Program." Paper presented at the Child Welfare League of America Conference, Washington, D.C., June 1984.

Rabin, Claire, Moshe Sens, and Hannah Rosenbaum. "Home-Based Marital Therapy for Multiproblem Families." *Journal of Marital and Family Therapy* 8, no. 4 (October 1982):451–461.

Reichler, Robert J., Haroutun M. Babigian, and Elmer A. Gardner. "The Mental Health Team: A Model for a Combined Community Approach to the Problems of Poor." *American Journal of Orthopsychiatry* 36 (April 1966):434–443.

Reid, William J., Richard M. Kagan, and Shirley B. Schlosberg. "Prevention of Placement: Critical Factors in Program Success." *Child Welfare* 67, no. 1 (January–February 1988):25–36.

Reynolds-Mejia, Patricia, and Sylvia Levitan. "Countertransference Issues in the In-Home Treatment of Child Sexual Abuse." *Child Welfare* 69, no. 1 (January–February 1990):53–61.

Riessman, Frank. "The 'Helper' Therapy Principle." *Social Work* 10, no. 2 (April 1965): 27–32.

———. "Strategies and Suggestions for Training Nonprofessionals." *Community Mental Health* 3, no. 2 (Summer 1967):103–110.

———. "New Approaches to Mental Health Treatment for Low-Income People." In *Interpersonal Helping: Emerging Approaches for Social Work Practice,* 529–544. Edited by Joel Fischer. Springfield, Ill.: Charles C. Thomas, 1973.

Robison, Susan. *Putting the Pieces Together: A Survey of State Systems for Children in Crisis.* Washington, D.C.: National Conference of State Legislatures, 1990.

Ronnau, John P. "A Strengths Approach to Helping Family Caregivers." *Children Today* 19, no. 6 (November–December 1990):24–27.

Ronnau, John P., and Alvin L. Sallee. "What's in a Name?" *National Association for Family-Based Services Newsletter* (Fall 1992):3.

Rosenblatt, Roger. "A Christmas Story," *Time,* December 30, 1985, 18–30.

Rosenthal, Perihan Aral, Susanne Mosteller, James L. Wells, and Ruick S. Rolland. "Family Therapy with Multiproblem, Multichildren Families in a Court Clinic Setting." *Journal of the American Academy of Child Psychiatry* 13, no. 1 (Winter 1974):126–142.

Sallee, Alvin L., and June C. Lloyd. *Family Preservation: Papers from the Institute for Social Work Educators 1990.* Riverdale, Ill.: National Association for Family-Based Services, 1991.

Sallee, Alvin L., and Marc Mannes. *Reflecting on the Past, Present and Future of the Family Preservation Movement.* Working Paper Series 1. Las Cruces, N.M.: Family Preservation Institute, Department of Social Work, New Mexico State University, 1991a.

———. *National Trends in Family Preservation: Implications for Region VI.* Working Paper Series Paper 2. Las Cruces, N.M.: Family Preservation Institute, Department of Social Work, New Mexico State University, 1991b.

———. *Infusing Family Preservation Values into Child Protection Practice.*

Working Paper Series Paper 3. Las Cruces, N.M.: Family Preservation Institute, Department of Social Work, New Mexico State University, 1992.

Samantri, Krishna. "To Prevent Unnecessary Separation of Children and Families: Public Law 96-272—Policy and Practice." *Social Work* 27, no. 4 (July 1992):295–302.

Sandau-Beckler, Pat. "Building Collaborative Relationships." *NAFBS Newsletter* (Winter–Spring 1993):2, 10.

Satir, Virginia. *Conjoint Family Therapy.* Palo Alto, Calif.: Science and Behavior Books, 1967.

Satir, Virginia. *Peoplemaking.* Palo Alto, Calif.: Science and Behavior Books, 1972.

Scales, Cynthia G. *Potato Chips for Breakfast: An Autobiography.* Stroudsburg, Pa.: Quotidian, 1986.

Schlachter, Roy H. "Home Counseling of Adolescents and Parents." *Social Work* 20, no. 6 (November 1975):427–428, 481.

Schlesinger, Benjamin. *The Multi-Problem Family: A Review and Annotated Bibliography.* Toronto: University of Toronto Press, 1963.

Schorr, Lisbeth, with Daniel Schorr. *Within Our Reach: Breaking the Cycle of Disadvantage.* Garden City, N.Y.: Anchor Press/Doubleday, 1988.

Schroeder, Carroll. "What Is 'Success?'" *NAFBS Newsletter* (National Association for Family-Based Services) (Summer 1992):3, 11.

Schuerman, John R., Tina L. Rzepnicki, Julia H. Littell, and Steve Budde. "Some Realities in the Implementation of Family Preservation Services." Prepared for the Conference on Child Welfare Reform Experiments, February 20–21, 1991, Washington, D.C. Chicago: Chapin Hall Center for Children, University of Chicago.

Seaberg, James. "'Reasonable Efforts': Toward Implementation in Permanency Planning." *Child Welfare* 65, no. 5 (September–October 1986):468–479.

———. "Family Policy Revisited: Are We There Yet?" *Social Work* 35, no. 6 (November 1990):548–554.

Segré, Jessica. "Children Respond to Emotionally Distressed Parents." *Parenting Professionals* (July 1993):2.

Select Committee on Children, Youth, and Families. U.S. House of Representatives. *No Place to Call Home: Discarded Children in America.* Washington D.C.: U.S. Government Printing Office, 1989.

Selig, Andrew L. "The Myth of the Multi-Problem Family." *American Journal of Orthopsychiatry* 46, no. 3 (July 1976):526–532.

Sgroi, Suzanne M., ed. *Vulnerable Populations.* Vol. 1: *Evaluation and Treatment of Sexually Abused Children and Adult Survivors.* New York: Lexington Books, 1989a.

———. *Vulnerable Populations.* Vol. 2: *Sexual Abuse Treatment for Chil-*

dren, Adult Survivors, Offenders, and Persons with Mental Retardation. New York: Lexington Books, 1989b.

Shure, Myrna B., and George Spivack. "Means-Ends Thinking, Adjustment and Social Class among Elementary School-Aged Children." *Journal of Consulting and Clinical Psychology* 38 (1972):348–353.

———. *Problem-Solving Techniques in Childrearing.* San Francisco: Jossey-Bass, 1978.

Simon, Richard. "Stranger in a Strange Land: An Interview with Salvador Minuchin." *Family Therapy Networker* 8, no. 6 (November–December 1984):20–31, 66–68.

———. "Across the Great Divide." *Family Therapy Networker* 10, no. 1 (January–February 1986):22–30, 74.

Slater, Edward P., and William R. Harris. "Therapy at Home." *Practice Digest* 1, no. 1 (June 1978):20–21.

Social Research Institute. University of Utah. "Analysis of Factors Contributing to the Failure of Family-Based Child Welfare Services." Draft. Salt Lake City, Utah, n.d.

Spivack, George, Jerome J. Platt, and Myrna B. Shure. *The Problem-Solving Approach to Adjustment.* San Francisco: Jossey-Bass, 1976.

Spivack, George, and Myrna B. Shure. *Social Adjustment of Young Children.* San Francisco: Jossey-Bass, 1974.

Stark, Evan, and Anne H. Flitcraft. "Women and Children at Risk: A Feminist Perspective on Child Abuse." *International Journal of Health Services* 18, no. 1 (1988):97–118.

Steele, William, and Melvyn Raider. *Working with Families in Crisis: School-Based Intervention.* Guilford Press, 1991.

Stehno, Sandra M. "Family-Centered Child Welfare Services: New Life for a Historic Idea." *Child Welfare* 65, no. 3 (May–June 1986):231–240.

———. "The Elusive Continuum of Child Welfare Services: Implications for Minority Children and Youths." *Child Welfare* 69, no. 6 (November–December 1990):551–562.

Stein-Cowan, Ellie. *Creating a Family-Based Service Delivery System.* Keynote speech, Massachusetts Department of Social Services, Empowering Families Symposium, Boston, February 3, 1992.

Steinmetz, Suzanne K., and Murray A. Straus, eds. *Violence in the Family.* New York: Harper & Row, 1974.

Stone, N. M., and Stone, S. F. "The Prediction of Successful Foster Placement." *Social Casework* 64, no. 1 (1983):11–17.

Straus, Murray. A., Richard Gelles, and Suzanne Steinmetz. *Behind Closed Doors: Violence in the American Family.* Garden City, N.Y.: Doubleday, 1980.

Stroul, Beth A. *Series on Community-Based Services for Children and Adolescents Who Are Severely Emotionally Disturbed.* Vol. 1: *Home-Based*

Services. Washington, D.C.: CASSP Technical Assistance Center, Georgetown University Child Development Center, 1988.

Sudia, Cecelia, "Family-Based Services: A Conference Report." *Children Today* 11, no. 5 (September–October 1982):12–13.

———. "Preventing Out-of-Home Placement of Children: The First Step for Permanency Planning." *Children Today* 15, no. 6 (November–December 1986):4–5.

———. "Drop 'Prevention' as Generic Description." *NAFBS Newsletter* (Winter–Spring 1993a):7–8, 11.

———. "The Origins and Development of Family-Based Services—From a Government Servant's Perspective." *Prevention Report* (Spring 1993b):4–6.

Sue, Derald Wing, and David Sue. *Counseling the Culturally Different: Theory and Practice.* 2d ed. New York: Wiley, 1990.

Sullivan, Maisha. "The Nguzo Saba: African-Centered Values as Tools for Family Assessment, Support, and Empowerment." *Family Resource Coalition Report* 12, no. 1 (Spring 1993):6–7.

Tannen, Naomi. "A Continuum of Home-Based Service." *Child Protection Connection* (November–December 1986).

———. "Entering Peoples Homes: Power/Humility." *Common Ground* 3, no. 2 (August 1987):1, 11.

———. "The Case for Long-Term Intervention in the Provision of Home-Based Services." In *Empowering Families: Papers from the Third Annual Conference on Family Based Services,* 45–50. Riverdale, Ill.: National Association for Family-Based Services, 1989.

Task Force on Successful Outcome in Family-Based Services. *Indicators of Successful Outcome in Family Preservation Services.* (Cedar Rapids, Iowa: National Association for Family-Based Services, n.d.).

Taylor, James B., and Martha Carithers. "Uses and Limits of Outreach Assessment." *Journal of Social Welfare* 3, no. 1 (Spring 1976):47–63.

Taylor, Joseph L. "The Child Welfare Agency as the Extended Family." *Child Welfare* 51, no. 2 (February 1972):74–83.

Taylor, Paul. "Programs Turn to Home As Children's Best Hope: Family-Preservation Movement Spreads." *Washington Post,* March 31, 1991.

Terr, Lenore. *Too Scared to Cry.* New York: Basic Books, 1990.

Thompson, Maxine Seaborn, and Wilma Peebles-Wilkins. "The Impact of Formal, Informal, and Societal Support Networks on the Psychological Well-Being of Black Adolescent Mothers." *Social Work* 37, no. 4 (July 1992):322–328.

Thorman, George. *Helping Troubled Families: A Social Work Perspective.* New York: Aldine, 1982.

Tollett, Erica E. "Public Policy and African American Families: Employment, Education, Community Development." *Family Resource Coalition Report* 12, no. 1 (Spring 1993):8–10.

Tracy, Elizabeth, M., Nadine Bean, Selma Gwatkin, and Barbara Hill. "Family Preservation Workers: Sources of Job Satisfaction and Job Stress." *Research on Social Work Practice* 2, no. 4 (October 1992):465–478.

Trepper, Terry S., and Mary Jo Barrett. *Treating Incest: A Multiple Systems Perspective.* New York: Haworth Press, 1986.

————. *Systemic Treatment of Incest: A Therapeutic Handbook.* New York: Brunner/Mazel, 1989.

Tyler, Margaret. *State Survey on Placement Prevention and Family Reunification Programs.* Iowa City: National Resource Center on Family Based Services, University of Iowa, December 1990.

Umbarger, Carter. "The Paraprofessional and Family Therapy." *Family Process* 11, no. 2 (June 1972):147–162.

Unger, Donald G. "Strengthening Youth and Family Resistance to Alcohol and Other Drug Abuse." *Family Resource Coalition Report* 10, no. 3 (1991):1–2.

University of Kentucky, College of Social Work. "Collaboration for Competency: Examining Social Work Curriculum in the Perspective of Current Practice with Children and Families." Lexington: University of Kentucky, 1989.

U.S. Advisory Board on Child Abuse and Neglect. *Creating Caring Communities: Blueprint for an Effective Federal Policy on Child Abuse and Neglect.* Washington, D.C.: U.S. Advisory Board on Child Abuse and Neglect, September 15, 1991.

————. *The Continuing Child Protection Emergency: A Challenge to the Nation.* Washington, D.C.: U.S. Advisory Board on Child Abuse and Neglect, April 1993.

U.S. Department of Health and Human Services. *Promising Practices: Reaching Out to Families.* Washington, D.C.: U.S. Department of Health and Human Services, May 1981.

U.S. Department of Health and Human Services. *Services Integration for Families and Children in Crisis.* San Francisco: U.S. Department of Health and Human Services, January 1991.

————. *Child Abuse and Neglect: A Shared Community Concern.* Washington, D.C.: U.S. Department of Health and Human Services, Revised March 1992.

U.S. General Accounting Office. *Home Visiting: A Promising Early Intervention Strategy for At-Risk Families.* Washington, D.C.: U.S. General Accounting Office, July 1990.

————. Human Resources Division. *Foster Care: Services to Prevent Out-of-Home Placements Are Limited by Funding Barriers.* Washington, D.C.: U.S. General Accounting Office, 1993.

Vanderbilt, Heidi. "Incest: A Chilling Report." *Lear's* (February 1992):51–77.

Vogel, Christine. "It Takes a Whole Village to Raise a Child." *Family Resource Coalition Report* 12, no. 1 (Spring 1993):15–17.

Walker, Lenore. *The Battered Woman.* New York: Harper & Row, 1979.

Walsh, Froma, ed. *Normal Family Processes.* New York: Guilford Press, 1982.

Warsh, Robin, Anthony Maluccio, and Barbara A. Pine. *Teaching Family Reunification: A Sourcebook.* Washington, D.C.: Child Welfare League of America, 1993.

Wasik, Barbara Hanna, Donna M. Bryant, and Claudia Lyons. *Home Visiting.* Newbury Park, Calif.: Sage, 1990.

Waxman, Laura DeKoven, and Deborah Frye. *A Status Report on Hunger and Homelessness in America's Cities: 1992, A 29-City Survey.* Washington, D.C.: U.S. Conference of Mayors, December 1992.

Waxman, Laura DeKoven, and Lilia M. Reyes. *A Status Report on Homeless Families in America's Cities: A 29-City Survey.* Washington, D.C.: U.S. Conference of Mayors, May 1987.

Wegscheider, Sharon. *Another Chance.* Palo Alto, Calif.: Science and Behavior Books, 1981.

Weikart, David P. "Quality Preschool Programs: A Long-Term Social Investment." New York: Ford Foundation, June 1989.

Weiss, Heather. "State Family Support and Education Programs: Lessons from Pioneers." *American Journal of Orthopsychiatry* 59, no. 1 (January 1989):32–48.

Weiss, Heather B., and Francine H. Jacobs, eds. *Evaluating Family Programs.* New York: Aldine de Gruyter, 1988.

Weissbord, Bernice. "The Maturing Family Support Movement: Shaping Practice and Policy for the '90s." *Family Resource Coalition Report* 7, no. 3 (1988):2–3.

Weissman, Harold H. *Integrating Services for Troubled Families: Dilemmas of Program Design and Implementation.* San Francisco: Jossey-Bass, 1978.

Wells, Kathleen, and David E. Biegel. "Intensive Family Preservation Services: Research Agenda for the 1990s." Paper presented at the Intensive

Family Preservation Services Research Conference, Cleveland, September 25–26, 1989.

———, eds. *Family Preservation Practice: Research and Evaluation*. Newbury Park, Calif: Sage, 1991.

Weston, Kath. *Families We Choose*. New York: Columbia University Press, 1991.

Whitaker, Carl A. *Midnight Musings of a Family Therapist*. New York: W. W. Norton, 1989.

Whitney, Pamela L., and Lonna Davis. "Child Abuse and Woman Abuse: Understanding the Connection and Designing Safe Interventions." *Common Ground* 10, no. 4 (November 1993):5.

Whittaker, James K. "Formal and Informal Helping in Child Welfare Services: Implications for Management and Practice." *Child Welfare* 65, no. 1 (January–February 1986):17–25.

Whittaker, James K., James Garbarino, and Associates. *Social Support Networks: Informal Helping in the Human Services*. New York: Aldine, 1983.

Whittaker, James K., Jill Kinney, Elizabeth M. Tracy, and Charlotte Booth, eds. *Reaching High-Risk Families: Intensive Family Preservation in Human Services*. New York: Aldine de Gruyter, 1990.

Wilson, Bette. "African American Academic Achievement: Issues, Answers, and Promising Strategies." *Family Resource Coalition Report* 12, no. 1 (Spring 1993):11–13.

Woititz, Janet. *Adult Children of Alcoholics*. Pompano Beach, Fla.: Health Communications, 1983.

Wolock, Isabel, Ludwig Geismar, Harriet Fink, and Barbara Dazzo. "Three Child Care Programs: A Comparative Study." *Australian Social Work* 32. no. 2 (June 1979):17–24.

Wood, Katherine M., and Ludwig L. Geismar. *Families at Risk: Treating the Multiproblem Family*. New York: Human Sciences Press, 1989.

Wood, Sally, and Keith Barton. "In-Home Treatment of Abusive Families: Cost and Placement at One Year." Davis, Calif.: Department of Applied Behavioral Sciences, University of California, August 1987.

Wood, Sally, Keith Barton, and C. Schroeder. "In-Home Treatment of Abusive Families: Cost and Placement at One Year." *Psychotherapy* 23, no. 3 (1988):409–414.

Woodbury, Michael A., and Margarita M. Woodbury. "Community-Centered Psychiatric Intervention: A Pilot Project in the 13th Arrondissement, Paris." *American Journal of Psychiatry* 126, no. 5 (November 1969):619–625.

Woods, Leonard J. "Home-Based Family Therapy." *Social Work* 33, no. 3 (May–June 1988):211–214.

Wylie, Mary Sykes. "The Evolution of a Revolution." *Family Therapy Networker* 16, no. 1 (January–February 1992):17–29, 98–99.

Yale University Bush Center in Child Development and Social Policy and Family Resource Coalition. *Programs to Strengthen Families: A Resource Guide.* New Haven: Yale University and Family Resource Coalition, 1983.

Yelton, Susan W. "Family Preservation from a Mental Health Perspective." *Child, Youth, and Family Services Quarterly* 14, no. 3 (Summer, 1991):6–8.

Yoast, Richard, and Kevin McIntyre. *Alcohol, Other Drug Abuse and Child Abuse and Neglect.* Madison: Wisconsin Clearinghouse, University of Wisconsin–Madison, 1991.

Yuan, Ying-ying T. "The Challenge of Evaluating Family Preservation Services Outcomes." *National Association for Family-Based Services Newsletter* (Fall 1992):7–8.

Yuan, Ying-ying T., Walter R. McDonald, C. E. Wheeler, D. Struckman-Johnson, and M. Rivest. "Evaluation of AB 1562 In-Home Care Demonstration Projects: Final Report." Sacramento, Calif.: Walter R. McDonald & Associates, May 1990.

Zalenski, John. "Creating Cultures of Family Support and Family Preservation: Four Case Studies." Iowa City: National Resource Center on Family-Based Services, 1993.

Zigler, Edward, and Susan Muenchow. *Head Start.* New York: Basic Books, 1992.

Index

About the Authors

Lisa Kaplan, ACSW, has devoted many years of work and study to the field of family treatment, focusing on high-risk families. She is Executive Director of Community Program Innovations, a national training center based in Danvers, Massachusetts. Community Program Innovations provides practical, hands-on training via workshops, conferences, and consultation. Lisa is the author of numerous publications on home-based, family-centered services. Her first book, *Working with Multiproblem Families,* was published in 1986.

Judith L. Girard, M.Ed., is Program Director of Taking Care of Business/ NUVA, a residential treatment program for homeless substance abusing women and their children in Gloucester, Massachusetts. Judy has many years of experience working with high-risk, multineed families. A single mother of three children and on welfare, Judy's children got involved with Head Start and she became an empowered Head Start parent. Thus began her career in family-centered services.